POLICY TRANSFER & EDUCATIONAL CHANGE

SAGE was founded in 1965 by Sara Miller McCune to support the dissemination of usable knowledge by publishing innovative and high-quality research and teaching content. Today, we publish over 900 journals, including those of more than 400 learned societies, more than 800 new books per year, and a growing range of library products including archives, data, case studies, reports, and video. SAGE remains majority-owned by our founder, and after Sara's lifetime will become owned by a charitable trust that secures our continued independence.

Los Angeles | London | New Delhi | Singapore | Washington DC | Melbourne

POLICY TRANSFER & EDUCATIONAL CHANGE

DAVID SCOTT, MAYUMI TERANO,
ROGER SLEE, CHRIS HUSBANDS
& RAPHAEL WILKINS

Los Angeles | London | New Delhi
Singapore | Washington DC | Melbourne

Los Angeles | London | New Delhi
Singapore | Washington DC | Melbourne

SAGE Publications Ltd
1 Oliver's Yard
55 City Road
London EC1Y 1SP

SAGE Publications Inc.
2455 Teller Road
Thousand Oaks, California 91320

SAGE Publications India Pvt Ltd
B 1/I 1 Mohan Cooperative Industrial Area
Mathura Road
New Delhi 110 044

SAGE Publications Asia-Pacific Pte Ltd
3 Church Street
#10-04 Samsung Hub
Singapore 049483

Editor: Marianne Lagrange
Editorial assistant: Robert Patterson
Production editor: Imogen Roome
Copyeditor: Christine Bitten
Proofreader: Bryan Campbell
Marketing manager: Dilhara Attygalle
Cover design: Naomi Robinson
Typeset by: C&M Digitals (P) Ltd, Chennai, India
Printed in India at Replika Press Pvt Ltd

© David Scott, Mayumi Terano, Roger Slee, Chris Husbands and Raphael Wilkins 2016

First published 2016

Apart from any fair dealing for the purposes of research or private study, or criticism or review, as permitted under the Copyright, Designs and Patents Act, 1988, this publication may be reproduced, stored or transmitted in any form, or by any means, only with the prior permission in writing of the publishers, or in the case of reprographic reproduction, in accordance with the terms of licences issued by the Copyright Licensing Agency. Enquiries concerning reproduction outside those terms should be sent to the publishers.

Library of Congress Control Number: 2015954639

British Library Cataloguing in Publication data

A catalogue record for this book is available from the British Library

ISBN 978-1-4739-1330-1
ISBN 978-1-4739-1331-8 (pbk)

At SAGE we take sustainability seriously. Most of our products are printed in the UK using FSC papers and boards. When we print overseas we ensure sustainable papers are used as measured by the PREPS grading system. We undertake an annual audit to monitor our sustainability.

CONTENTS

Preface vi
Acknowledgements ix

1 Introduction 1
2 India and its System of Education 14
3 The Spread of Ideas 27
4 Teachers as Professional Learners 37
5 School Autonomy and School Leadership 59
6 Inclusive Practices 86
7 Policy Learning 109

References 123
Author Index 131
Subject Index 133

Preface

This important and, I hope, influential book is about how ideas travel within countries and round the world. The principal theme is reforming school systems, and in the book we examine how efforts in India to achieve this were generally unsuccessful. In particular, we concentrate on the means to achieve this, i.e. the use of a policy-borrowing model, whereby exemplary practices developed in countries round the world are transferred to a recipient country, such as India, our case study. In the end we suggest that this policy-borrowing model is both flawed conceptually and in addition, failed in practice. We have therefore suggested a different model, which we have called a policy-learning model, that is, identifying a set of practices which are considered to be successful in one national setting and then transposing them to another national setting, in which a problem or need has been identified. In order to solve this problem or meet this need, policy-makers and practitioners learn from practices developed in other countries. The focus and the underlying methodology are not arbitrarily chosen from an infinite assortment of possible focuses and methodologies. Their use therefore has to be justified; a task that we undertake in this book.

Our purpose then, is to develop and articulate a comparative methodology which allows us to understand how educational ideas travel and subsequently influence classroom practices. What this means is that a binding, sufficient and salient reason (or reasons) has to be provided as to why our theory of policy learning is better than other theories focusing on the same area of social life. A number of arguments have been put forward as to whether it is possible to show that $Theory_1$ is better than $Theory_2$, and indeed whether this in principle can be achieved.

The first of these is that there are real issues which impact on our lives and it is these real issues that determine the truthfulness of particular theories. This is an argument in support of ontological realism but it doesn't take us very far in establishing whether it is possible to determine that one theory is better than another. However, what it does do is indicate that one of our criteria for this determination is related to the referent of knowledge (indeed that knowledge does have a referent). This is an important step in the argument for judgemental rationality (our ability to decide that one theory is better than another when they are both focused on the same area of social life), but it is not sufficient in itself to establish categorically that it is possible.

A second argument is that inevitably we do make judgements and we need to make them wisely. This is a curious argument and it suggests, in a tentative fashion, a foundational move. However, this argument is simply another way of asserting that it is possible to make these judgements. It doesn't provide us with the means to make such judgements. Another attempt is to suggest that the categories we use in the world are open to change. This is simply a reiteration of the central claim that our knowledge–development activity is located in specific geo-social-historical locations.

The most promising argument in favour of judgemental rationality is that once it has been established that ontological realism is a truthful claim, then what follows from this is that there is a relation/connection between knowledge development and the world (not of course in a correspondence or representational sense). This means that it then becomes possible to produce knowledge of this connection/relation and of the world itself, even if it is indirect. If in relation to the comparative methodology that we have chosen and judged to be superior to other comparative methodologies, we can show how it works, then we can begin the work of grounding our theories in the world as it is and thus establishing in part the possibility of claiming that T_1 is better than T_2.

Another argument is that if one theory can explain more significant phenomena than another, then it is a superior theory. However, this seemingly persuasive argument needs to be clarified. What exactly does it mean? Clearly if there are anomalies, contradictions or inadequacies in T_1, then it becomes possible for us to argue that this theory is inadequate or insufficient. So in trying to determine whether it is possible to establish that T_1 is superior to T_2 then we also (in addition to our epistemic criterion) have to build in a notion of rational adequacy. However, I don't think that there is a problem in using these two criteria together in any judgement we might want to make between T_1 and T_2.

A fifth argument that would allow us to make a judgement between two different theories about the same object of investigation is that if one accepts that experiments can provide knowledge, then logically it becomes possible to accept ontological realism. I think that this is a strong claim; however, it is not a sufficient argument for establishing that T_1 is superior to T_2.

A further argument refers to Jurgen Habermas' notion of communicative competence. The argument would then be that T_1 is superior to T_2 because in its production it better conforms to the rules for communicative competence. That is, any claim to theoretical credibility must be able to make the following assertions: this work is intelligible and hence meaningful in the light of the structuring principles of its discourse community; what is being asserted propositionally is true; what is being explained can be justified; and the person who is making these claims is sincere about what they are asserting. These four conditions if they are fulfilled allow a theorist to say something meaningful about the world. However, since we are trying to establish whether it is possible to determine that T_1 is superior to T_2, then we cannot use the argument that T_1 is superior on the grounds that the supporter of T_1 is coming from a better or purer position than the supporter of T_2, because this assumes that the argument being made is necessarily right.

It is suggested that another way of determining whether T_1 is superior to T_2 is to make the claim that T_1 is more powerful and has more powerful effects than other theories, for example, T_2, T_3, through to T_n. Self-evidently, some interpretations are more powerful or have more powerful effects in the world than others; however, this cannot provide us with an argument that might suggest that it is possible to say that T_1 is a better theory qua its theoretical adequacy than T_2.

What are we left with? There are four ways of distinguishing between different theories or models. The first is epistemic: a theory is superior to another because it is more empirically adequate. The second is the converse, so that a version of reality is superior to another because it contains fewer contradictions, disjunctions and aporias. A third approach focuses on the giving of reasons, and concludes that some reasons and systems of rationality are superior to others, and therefore should be preferred. A fourth approach is pragmatic: a theory is better than another because it is more practically adequate or referenced to/part of extant frameworks of meaning. A combination of all four reasons is appropriate. What we have attempted to do then in this book is provide a reason or set of reasons as to why our comparative methodology is superior to other methodologies that have been developed by other people.

David Scott

September 2015

Acknowledgements

The authors would like to acknowledge the contribution of Charles Posner, Chris Martin and Elsa Gusman to pages 1–4 of this book.

1
INTRODUCTION

Since the development of human capital theory with its ambitious and far-reaching claims to have identified a significant correlation between education and economic achievement, we have witnessed an unprecedented bevy of educational reforms, particularly in the developing world. These reforms have largely concentrated on curricular and workforce changes using evaluation processes and techniques, supposedly premised on national and international research findings. To the extent that the mechanisms responsible for implementing these innovations and changes are referred to, it is assumed that their success depends on a well-ordered and functioning educational administration free from interference. Superficially this has meant, firstly, paying lip service to the mantra that business models of management provide sufficient leverage to override 'outside interference', and secondly, it has been predicated on the unarticulated belief that national administrations are both efficient and neutral. However, this model has never operated in practice and the reforms both good and bad have rarely been successfully implemented.

This book examines the reasons for India's failure to bring these generally excellent proposals for reform and improvement to fruition. On the one hand, India has been particularly open to the suggestions and urgings of international organisations as to how to improve its educational performance. Yet, on the other, its system of administration vital to the possible success of implementing these reforms is closed and driven by internal conflict that has continuously paralysed all hope of delivery and effectively cancelled out changes initiated at the top level or originating from official international consultancies in which researchers from all over the world have often played an important role.

Obviously, these sometimes bewildering changes and processes have not enjoyed a good reception. Indian teachers and particularly those who have been in service over this entire period of frequent and hectic reform and who are on the receiving end of these initiatives, when asked what they think of them, interestingly comment much less on the actual content of the reforms, than on processes and their outcomes. A frequently expressed view is 'the more it all changes, the more it stays the same'. Questions we need to ask are why, and hence how, do costly reforms fail in India, and what lessons for other countries can be drawn from an analysis of those experiences? What can our understanding of the reasons for the continual failure of reforms tell us about how to make them more effective? In other words, how can one rescue the core elements of useful reforms to make them reach, and work better at, the level of the school? These are the questions we will try to answer in this book.

It should be apparent that, to a large extent, we are referring to the failure to implement policy. Generally speaking the failure to implement a policy is often attributed to four major factors: the design of the policy itself is flawed (it is not coherent, well-directed and practical and does not mesh with others operating in the same field); the policy is politically and/or socially unacceptable; insufficient attention is paid to the process of communicating and delivering the policy; and there are inadequate conditions in the classroom and for the preparation of teachers in the implementation of the policy.

In order to address these impediments or failures to successful implementation it is necessary to address four facets or dimensions of the problem. The first of these is the structure of any new programme, i.e. its comprehensiveness, coherence and relevance. The new programme is composed of a set of elements arranged in a logically coherent way, i.e. arrangements of resources, functions and roles for stakeholders, and vertical and horizontal relationships between these allocations of resources, functions and roles. The programme has a causal narrative, that is, the productive practice, the focus of the reform, is such that a leads to b; or the implementation of a in ideal circumstances leads to b_1, b_2, b_3 and so on. And the programme has a comprehensive and appropriate rationale (ethical, practical and consequential) and a realistic implementation plan. For example, in relation to pre-service and in-service teacher training curricula, it is important to develop a comprehensive set of curriculum standards and learning outcomes, syllabus content that extends from subject knowledge to developmental processes, a coherent structure of pedagogic standards or teaching and learning arrangements, and a strategy for involving educational reformers, policy developers and jurisdictional authorities in the process from the outset.

The second facet or dimension refers to the sites of implementation, how they are constructed and how they functioned prior to the new reform. The third dimension refers to how the current implementation site would need to be changed to accommodate the new initiative, and the fourth refers to issues of institutional structure, form and capacity at these sites. It is in the last of these – the institutional capacity – that we come across an issue that is rarely discussed in the relevant literature. In the literature on school improvement there are many examples of initiatives that flourished while support was being provided by an external agency or research team, but that withered when the external support ended, practice reverting to the status quo ante. Creating change in organisations is a complicated business, given that an organisational culture often exerts controls and deters change.

By institutionalisation we mean the degree to which the central activities, aptitudes and attitudes of the intervention become embedded in the structures and culture of the school, pervading the thinking and actions of teachers, administrators and students. Institutionalisation of the intervention is not guaranteed; the literature on organisational development and school reform suggests that there is a wide range of conditions in schools that can positively or negatively impact on the take-up, spread and depth of any reform, and that these conditions interact with one another and with reform efforts in complex, interactive ways.

Administrative Inertia

Writers who deal with institutional incapacity, and international and national policy-makers, refer to staff training and administrative reorganisation as if they are dealing exclusively with a technical problem that can easily be resolved by making the administration more responsive. Undeniably administration inertia is a problem because, by nature, administrations are resistant to change. To a certain extent, the modus operandi is to treat policy initiatives as occupational hazards to be neutralised as quickly and effectively as possible. However, the problem is more complex because administrations do not function in a void. They are predicated on social systems and processes that contextualise their work, including specific sets of epistemological perspectives, and these same systems, knowledge sets and processes are influential at every stage of implementation. This means that the administration is a reflection and a projection of the social order and must be understood as such.

What this means is that the comparative unresponsiveness of the bureaucracy to policy-making in developing countries is especially marked due, in part, to the relatively recent development of public systems of administration and the relatively late development of educational systems and their consolidation of the apparatus to implement policy. It may well be the case that the staff is insufficiently trained and administrative procedures and regulations are weak. In this sense we can talk about insufficient institutionalisation because the organisation cannot count on adequate human resources and administrative coherence. But institutionalisation goes beyond these aspects that are readily susceptible of technical resolution, that is, more training and bureaucratic reorganisation. Institutionalisation includes the degree to which the organisation manages to communicate its purpose and identity to its staff and its identity is more often than not distorted by the needs and actions of interest groups. The staff, in turn, respond to the incentives and sanctions that the institution operates in order to achieve its purposes. This is an important theme but it is only one aspect of a more general problem.

The crux of the matter is that the administrations of most developing countries are markedly different from the administrations of more developed countries with their strong historically entrenched independent identities. The state apparatus in emerging political entities is likely to be under the control of the political groups or coalitions of interest currently exercising power and is often a site of both conflict and compromise amongst them. Its primary function is one of attenuation or control of the conflicts, the search for compromise and the control of the population as a whole. Under these circumstances the obstacles to an independent identity to carry out its designated purpose – education in our case – is severely circumscribed by what we can call power politics. This is especially true in India, where political stability has been achieved through corporate integration of all the major sectors and strata of the society. It has not been achieved by direct political control as in authoritarian states; neither have the counterbalances from plural democracies kept a watchful eye on the bureaucracy's accomplishment of its designated purposes. Indian corporative politics puts general loyalty to groups and individuals over and above the specific purposes of the organisations in which they operate.

Bureaucracies then, are also sites where political leaders and groups can provide positions for their supporters. To put it another way, the primary purpose of the educational administration is not to develop and/or implement educational policies, but to position leaders and groups using appropriate mechanisms to do so. In this sense the problem of reform implementation is not one of incapacity or disorganisation or of a lack of institutionalisation but an inability to focus on the prime concerns of an education system. Once we recognise that a significant part of the failure of policy to reach the schools successfully intact is the very modus vivendi of the administration itself, then it is equally clear that solutions will be difficult to find. Any attempt to instil the improvements contemplated within policies would involve challenging established institutional behaviours. This in turn would depend on the corporative distribution of personal and group loyalties changing, something we unfortunately and frustratingly are unlikely to see in the near future.

In this book we are interested in all aspects of policy implementation: pedagogical, organisational, resourcing and political–institutional. Critical accounts of policy developments and policy implementations in India will be used to demonstrate that we take particularly seriously the hitherto neglected category of institutional and political infrastructure. But at every point our examination of the non-educational (political) aspects of the bureaucracy will point to the desired educational outcomes and the failure or success of bringing these about.

Education Policy

It is important to start with a framework for educational implementation, a check list of necessary elements and steps that condition and contextualise the processes of implementation. More recent education policy researchers, such as Stephen Ball (1994), depict curriculum reform and policy-making as a 'messy', complex and contested enterprise. As has been frequently observed (for example, Whitty, 2002), policy is an object of contest and struggle between competing ideologies, education visions, personal interests and political or organisational positions. All of these forces come together in an incubator of international, national and local contexts. For Ball, understanding education reforms requires us to interrogate policy cycles, policy discourses, policy actors, policy arenas and contexts. His is a nuanced and more realistic approach to analysing education reform developed over years through a series of empirical analyses of policy sites, discourses and contexts. Policy is produced through a series of struggles involving many actors and agencies. In addition, local policy cannot be understood without reference to the global impact of transnational agencies such as the Organisation for Economic Cooperation and Development (OECD), the United Nations Educational Scientific and Cultural Organisation (UNESCO), the United Nations Children's Fund (UNICEF), the World Bank, not for profit and for profit organisations, and so forth.

Change to an education system and its curriculum is always a change to the status quo, to what already exists. Therefore in trying to understand how national education systems and their curricula change, it is important to understand how those systems and curricula are currently structured. What this means is that the same programme of reform delivered in different countries is likely to have different effects on the different elements of the system and will have different histories within the system. It is possible to categorise reform effect and history in five ways: point of entry into the system and direction of flow, sustainability of the integrity of the reform, intensity of the reform or capacity to effect change, malleability of the system or capacity to change, and institutionalisation processes.

With regards to the first of these – point of entry and direction of flow – there are a number of possible scenarios. There are different points of entry: at the top of the system where this is understood either as the progenitor of policy or as the apex of a power structure however diffuse it is or becomes; at the bottom of the system so that the point of entry is not at the political, policy-making, bureaucratic or official level but at the level of teacher and classroom; or at a variety of entry points in the system. Broadly, three models depicting direction of flow can be identified: a centrally controlled policy process where the direction is uni-directional and downward oriented; a pluralist model where the direction of flow is still uni-directional, but the developmental movement is to all parts of the system and the orientation is pluralist; and a fragmented and multi-directional model where new policy (which represents the reform) is always in a state of flux as policy texts are received and interpreted at different points in the system and the process is understood as fragmented, non-linear, contested and as a place where original intentions are rarely fulfilled in practice. In other words, without a consistent flow that is distributed throughout the system, there will always be an element of risk involved that the reform will result in unintended outcomes.

The second of these elements is the sustainability of the integrity of the reform over time. What we mean by this is the capacity of the reform to retain its original shape, form and content as it is disseminated through the system. A reform is embedded in what already exists. Most obviously the reform itself as it was originally conceived (in its pure and ideal state) undergoes processes of amendment, modification, correction and revision, and it does this at different points in the process. These different points can be described as: exploration and development, recontextualisation, implementation, re-implementation and institutionalisation. When we refer to the integrity of a reform, this should not be understood in any ideal or absolute sense. A reform or an intervention in a system is always an amalgam of different ideas and prescriptions that is never completely coherent. What can be suggested, however, is that in the long process of formulation of the reform to application, to implementation, and thence to institutionalisation, the original integrity of the reform is either strongly or weakly maintained.

The third feature is the intensity of the reform (or intervention) and its capacity to effect change. This refers to the structure of the reform or the way it is constituted. Some reforms are focused on relations within the system that are likely to have a minimal impact on the system as a whole; others aim to influence the whole workings of the system. Examples of the former include labour market reforms, which though they usually come within a package of other reforms, are designed to impact on one part of the system and not the whole. On the other hand, reforms, for example, which focus on the curriculum and the way it is delivered, as in the 1988 Education Reform Act in the United Kingdom, which changed the whole tenor and orientation of education in that country, can be thought of as whole system reforms or interventions. Furthermore, some of these reforms are crafted so that, even given the state of the system into which they are being introduced, they have a more fundamental impact than other reforms. This in turn points to the degree of resilience of the system or capacity to resist a reform. And, indeed, any educational system has a limited capacity to resist being reformed, not least because those elements that allow it to resist may be the objective of the reform; systems therefore have a greater or lesser capacity to resist reforms. Equally, a reform itself has a greater or lesser capacity to impact on and change the structures and environments into which it is being introduced, and in part this refers to not only how it is going to be introduced, but also to the structures and constitution of the reform package itself. Its penetrative power (though this may not be realised) or capacity to effect change is different with different reforms. This is the intensity of the reform or intervention, and clearly its obverse is the resilience or otherwise of the current arrangements within the system. This is the malleability of that system.

Beyond this, there are institutionalising elements in the system, two of which are particularly important. The first of these is the longevity and sustainability of resource arrangements, allocations of particular people to positions of responsibility, particular roles and arrangements of power and authority, and the capacity of key people in the system, new policy discourses, new policies and new priorities. The second element is the capacity to adapt to changes to these new policy discourses, policies and priorities. An example of an institutionalised mechanism set up to allow this to happen is a formal curriculum review at a set point in time, though most educational processes of review, development and implementation round the world are conducted on an ad hoc basis; when, where and how are decided by political imperatives.

Education Reforms

Insight into problems faced by an educational system and awareness of potential solutions do not necessarily lead to the ability to act in an effective manner in order to guide stakeholders in instituting change. The rapid and successful implementation of education reforms in a school system is directly dependent on the quality of the knowledge, skills and thinking that an education system and those that introduce its planned reforms bring to the reform process. Moreover, innovations and reforms call for new and often substantially improved, knowledge, skills and thinking in several domains. This includes knowledge about obstacles to change at both the instrumental and affective levels and about the change process itself.

John Kotter (2012) suggests eight steps that characterise effective change: establishing a legitimate sense of urgency; creating a guiding coalition with enough power and knowledge to lead the change; developing a strategy and a vision; communicating the change vision; empowering broad-based action; generating short-term wins and celebrating them; consolidating gains and producing more change; and anchoring these new approaches in the work culture. Kotter warns that it is particularly in the later stages of a change process when progress is being made toward achieving goals that change is likely to fail because people are then often tired and feel enough has been accomplished. If planned changes are not sufficiently integrated with organisational routines, they tend to dissipate. Applying Kotter's eight steps is far from being a simple mechanistic process. It requires a solid knowledge about communications, planning, stakeholder inclusion, knowledge management and the development of systems, as well as commitment to the planned change. In addition, he also stresses the need for planned changes to appeal as much to the heart as the mind. Kotter further argues that in times of accelerated change, organisations need two systems that operate in concert: traditional hierarchies and flexible networks staffed with people from the whole of the organisation who are empowered to propose and lead change. What is also needed is an extensive understanding of the way the potential model of reform, for example, when it refers to teacher training or inclusive practices or devolved governance, works as an abstract model, in practices external to the reform setting, and potentially in practices in the reform setting, such as Indian teacher training institutes, schools and colleges.

Michael Fullan (2007) in turn, proposes a different set of reform elements: maintaining a focus on moral purpose; understanding change; increasing coherence among various aspects of a planned change; relationship-building; knowledge creation and sharing; and building commitment among an organisation's internal and external members (i.e. its stakeholders). Fullan focuses on consciously being aware of shaping and using the ideational realm of aspirations, commitment and values, as well as the mechanics of how people work together, create and manage knowledge. His work suggests that particular care has to be given to ensure that various documents, be these vision statements, plans or policies, are aligned with one another so each supports the other, and core messages and directions are clear to those reading and implementing the documents. Again, in this model there is a neglect of the relevance of internal elements of the specific reform and the relations between them.

Fullan (2014) argues that Ontario was successful in reforming its education system partly because it used positive as opposed to negative pressure. Fullan defines positive pressure as being characterised by having the system maintain a focus on urgency, building partnerships and working with peers, making key data openly available and instituting non-punitive accountability, all the while seeking to create irresistible synergy. As with any model, the Ontario model may appear attractive due to its simplicity, but caution is also required. Ontario experienced numerous problems which have not been fully explored such as the negative backwash effects of examinations; moreover, whilst it clearly demonstrated the capacity of a system to adapt to policy change, there remain significant elements of under-performance which were not addressed. Even allowing the success of the Ontario approach, it does not follow that Fullan provides a clear blue-print which can be replicated elsewhere; contexts are distinctive in an ever-changing world.

However, despite what is now known about successful educational change, it is noteworthy that education systems and their institutional arrangements are stubbornly resistant to change. Two central messages about overcoming resistance to change arise out of the work of leading thinkers in change management. The first is that those leading change require high levels of meta-cognitive, meta-affective and meta-social awareness. The second is that people approach change with their personal understandings and feelings, and that these need to be explored in relationship to work in order to understand their impact on the work process. In other words, change in and of education systems almost always requires more than mechanical or technical solutions. Whatever changes are sought, usually these also need to lead to a change in beliefs, feelings, knowledge and behaviours, if a change is to be sustainable.

Normally when a government decides to reform its education system, or any other public service for that matter, it begins by examining what is on offer, and then selects what fits best in relation to its political leanings and the various constraints within which it operates. Although it is important to distinguish these approaches in order to clarify their potential to reach particular educational goals, their incarnation in real-life settings is what determines what happens in the final instance. Social participation in the United Kingdom during the 1980s had different meanings and outcomes to that experienced in Nicaragua in the same period. Sometimes policies may grow organically out of previous ones or cohere easily with others in other sectors, but elsewhere they may be superimposed on, or make a sharp break with, what previously existed, and may be assembled in an incoherent fashion, clashing with other education or economic policies.

Reform Models

Currently on offer are four basic approaches to educational reform. The first of these is a top-down model. Governments stipulate the types of judgement that should be made about the successful delivery of educational policies, and about how this should be achieved. They have the resources to impose these reforms on the system, though this is rarely achieved in practice in ways that policy-makers intended. The reason for this is that reform processes are generally multi-directional rather than uni-directional. Policy texts and directives issued by governments always allow amendments and changes to be made at every stage of the process and at every level (including the stages of implementation). This more fluid model of policy better reflects the relationship between policy development and implementation. A variant on this is an evaluative state model where the state withdraws from the precise implementation of policy though it clearly has an important role in framing that policy. It sets up a series of semi-independent bodies whose purpose is to ensure that institutions and individuals conform to government directives. These semi-independent bodies have a role in interpreting government policy and subsequently enforcing these policies by imposing sanctions on institutions and individuals if they do not conform. The reform process is carried out by quasi-government agencies at arm's length from governments. This is however, still very much a top-down reform model.

A second type is the quasi-market model. Here, governments decide to withdraw directly from the formation and implementation of policy, and set up quasi-market systems which hand power to the consumer, thus putting pressure on educational institutions by either exercising or threatening to exercise powers of voice or exit. If in the latter case too much of this takes place, then this threatens the survival of the organisation. The market is a quasi-market, not least because some groups of consumers have a greater capacity to exercise voice or exit, and therefore have a greater degree of cultural capital and can display and use it more effectively than other people.

A third reform model is the professional development model. Here it is thought that different types of decisions within a system should be made by different people, because at the level at which they operate they are more likely to have the required expertise for making such decisions. Professional interests therefore drive this reform process.

The final model is the social participation model, and the principle underpinning this is that since there are no conclusive ways of determining the correctness of particular sets of values, decisions within education systems have to be made through negotiations between the various stakeholders. This means that no particular stakeholder has a monopoly of power over any other, or can claim a special status, but the various partners negotiate with each other and come to an agreed solution. What this also means is that the method for reaching agreement has to be in some ideal sense divested of those power relations which privilege one stakeholder over another.

In trying to understand how interventions in education systems work, in the first instance we need to remind ourselves of the principal elements of a public educational practice, namely, that it comprises the state's deployment of human resources, its strategic hold over infrastructure and other material and financial resources, its mobilisation of ceremonies, rituals, meanings and values, and its creation and maintenance of a central value system. Therefore, in trying to understand how national education systems, such as the Indian system and its curriculum, change, we need to understand how the Indian system and its curriculum are currently structured. Thus, the same programme of reform delivered in different countries is likely to have different effects on the different elements of the system and will have different histories within the system. What we have been identifying here are internal relations in a change process.

There are also exogenous or extra-national influences, although we have to be clear that these globalising pressures do not determine policy and practice within particular countries in an over-arching way. Globalisation comprises a process of policy and practice convergence between different nations, regions and jurisdictions in the world. This can occur in a number of ways. The first is through a process of policy borrowing or policy learning, where the individual country is the recipient of policies from other countries or from a collection of other countries. These processes impact in complex ways on educational practices, and not only on state-sponsored ones. The second is through the direct impact of supranational bodies which have power and influence over member countries and which are seeking harmonisation of national educational policies and practices. The third is a more subtle approach and this is where the supra-national body does not deal in policies or practices but in a common currency of comparison, which may be epistemic (as in the means used by, for example, the OECD to compare one education system with another) or functional (as in the distribution of resources, including discursive resources). The fourth process that potentially allows convergence is the autochthonous response of each national system of education to a common imperative from outside its jurisdiction, though in most cases this is more likely to encourage divergence rather than convergence. The fifth is a direct response to globalisation pressures by a nation, region or jurisdiction. With regards to the influence and impact of globalisation, there are four possible spatio-temporal positioners: the extension and extensive capacity of the global network, its intensity, the velocity of the global flows and the impact they are likely to have (cf. Held et al., 1999). We address these issues at a later stage in this book, where we examine these globalising imperatives and influences through such notions as policy transfer and policy learning, and in particular, in our analysis, borrow a notion of vernacular globalisation from Lingard (2000), which pays careful attention to national, regional and jurisdictional autochthonous responses to the various forms of globalisation that currently exist.

Policy Learning

This book focuses on the important notion of policy learning. We offer here some comments on this approach. Our concern then, is with policy learning, i.e. identifying a set of practices which are considered to be successful in one national setting and then transposing them to another national setting (as we have already indicated, the example we use in this book is India), in which a problem or need has been identified; and the policy which has been transposed is thought to be a solution to the problem or able to meet this need, with the transfer understood as a learning activity.

Policy borrowing in one variant (P_1) has a series of stages, as in the model developed by Phillips and Schweisfurth (2008): conceptualisation (neutralising the questions to be addressed), contextualisation (providing a description of the issues against local backgrounds in two or more of the cases), isolation of differences (determining variances), explanation (developing an hypothesis), reconceptualisation (contextualising the findings) and application (generalising the findings).

This model can be usefully amended (i.e. to P_2) so that it now includes seven steps or phases. The first step is where the investigator conceptualises the focus of the investigation. She then identifies a mechanism within Country A (where this is the country from which the policy is being borrowed). A third step is understanding how this mechanism works in the context of Country A; in other words, identifying those factors within Country A which allow the mechanism to work as it was intended or at least as it has been adapted to a new set of circumstances (over time but still within Country A). A fourth step is identifying another country (B) which seems to be a suitable recipient of this mechanism, that is, it seems to have some similarities to the donor's context. A fifth step is identifying those similarities and differences between the contexts of the two countries. A sixth step is making a judgement about the degree of similarity and difference between the two settings and subsequently making a judgement about the amount and type of change required for the mechanism to work in Country B, which also requires a judgement to be made about whether the mechanism is working or not; this involves predicting how one mechanism which seems to work in one particular socio-historical setting should work in another which is characterised by a different set of organisational arrangements. And finally, having identified the consequences of transferring the mechanism to the new country, the policy transfer is implemented.

A third model (P_3), and the one which we will be developing in this book, is a policy-learning model, and it therefore has built into it the characteristics of a learning process. An accepted, but not uncontested, view of learning is to theorise it as a process, with a range of characteristics. It has a set of pedagogic relations, that is, it incorporates a relationship between a learner and a catalyst, which could be a person, a text, an object in nature, a particular array of resources, an educational system or process, an artefact, an allocation of a role or function to a person, or a sensory object. A change process is required, either internal to the learner or external to the community of which this learner is a member. In any learning episode, there are temporal and spatial arrangements, and these can be understood in two ways: first, that learning is internally structured, and second, that learning episodes are externally located in time and space.

The first policy-borrowing model (P_1) is focused on the transformation of one set of descriptors about a policy mechanism into another so that the second set now fits the new circumstances in which the policy will be enacted. Here the contrastive assumption is that generalised knowledge can be produced through a process of identifying similarities and differences between a phenomenon and the circumstances in which it can be applied, and eliminating those factors that are not relevant to the transformative process. In the second policy-borrowing model (P_2 adapted from P_1) there is a further assumption made that those descriptors refer to real events, happenings and mechanisms, and thus the transformational process has as its product a transformation of a material reality. The third and more significant model (P_3) builds in an element of learning into the process and thus contextualises such learning both at the site of formation and at the site of implementation of the recipient country.

Productive Practices

In this book, we focus on productive practices that could and did form the centrepiece for educational reforms in our case study country, India. The development of these productive practices formed the major part of a research and development project conducted by us and in conjunction with Save-the-Children, India, and funded by the European Union. We refer to the project's aims, activities and outputs throughout, and in particular in the concluding chapter we attempt to show why the envisaged purposes of the reform processes in the end were frustrated. In the first place, we identified jurisdictions (for example, Finland, England and Australia) that were thought likely to be *productive locations for learning* in relation to teacher cadre management systems, including teacher selection, recruitment and preparation. We also examined issues relating to school autonomy, school management and decentralisation, and identified jurisdictions that had a reputation for innovative practices in this area. The third productive practice we identified was removing barriers to inclusive education. This reform concentrated on India's efforts to improve educational and social outcomes for all their students. Particular attention was paid to inclusive education reform initiatives that allow the inclusion of vulnerable students such as indigenous students, and policies and programmes that dealt with a range of issues of student displacement through poverty, family migration, the education of refugee children and the girl child. Also foregrounded were recent approaches to the education of children with disabilities.

These three areas are the three productive practices in the book, reflecting our concern that the focus needs to be on how practitioners and policy-makers learn from the work and experience of each other, rather than on the apparently exemplary practice itself. Therefore, we do not see learning from international comparative experience as a passive process of policy borrowing. Because we saw the jurisdictions from which the three productive practices emerged as productive locations for learning, the effectiveness of the transfer depended to some extent not on the practices adopted in the countries studied, but on the quality of the learning derived from them and the way that learning played out in practice in the new environment. This is a process which needs to be actively managed with close attention to contextual specificities, cultural divergences and the dilemmas of globalising education policy. The focus here is on generative practices rather than on generalising educational practices across very different contexts.

We identify key initiatives within the three themed areas and have produced a detailed narrative about each of these three productive practices (see Chapters 4, 5 and 6). This allowed us to demonstrate the thinking behind the productive practice, its context and impacts, and further allowed us to understand not only the quality and properties of the chosen initiatives, but also the processes through which they could be successfully implemented. This represents the essence of policy learning. In the next chapter we examine the site of implementation for our three productive practices, India and its education system.

2

INDIA AND ITS SYSTEM OF EDUCATION

In the previous chapter we identified three productive practices relating to teacher development, devolved governance and inclusive practices. The development of these productive practices formed the major part of a research and development project, undertaken by us and in conjunction with a leading non-governmental organisation (NGO) in India which we have already referred to and will continue to do so in the rest of the book. We also identified four components of a reform programme: the constitution of the reform, the sites of implementation and how they functioned prior to the implementation of the new reform, understandings about what would need to be changed in order to accommodate the new reform programme, and its institutionalisation. The site of implementation in our case study and the recipient of the productive practices is India and its system of education. In this chapter we explore the historical, structural, relational and discursive elements of this important and massive education system.

It is customary to speak of modern mass education as a *system* and indeed there is a great deal of sense in this for the reasons we explain below. However, describing education as a system risks ignoring the core of that activity, namely, that it is a series of profoundly personal acts of learning. Thus from the outset, any consideration of education needs to take into account the tension between the instinctive drive to learn and the systematic attempt to organise and control it. The root of this tension lies in the difference between the basic demand for access to learning opportunities for the satisfaction of needs (emotional, spiritual, material and intellectual) and the control and selection processes that education systems undertake. As a result, in all societies there is a dissonance between neo-liberal rationality and broader social democratic progress.

Whether change occurs or not depends on the capacity within the system as well as the condition of the change-catalyst or set of reforms. And these in turn are structured in particular ways, which determine their ability to act as change agents. As we have suggested, certain types of catalyst are more likely to induce change in a system than others; for example, changes of personnel (caused naturally through retirements and deaths or by people in powerful positions within the system exercising their authority), new policies, events in nature, external interventions, new arrays of resources, new arrangements of roles and functions within a system, new financial settlements and so forth, have different capacities to effect change in an education system. In short, some of these change catalysts are more powerful than others, or at least have the potential to be more powerful. Even here though, the capacity of the catalyst to effect change within a system does not guarantee or determine whether change actually occurs. Self-evidently, it does not guarantee or determine the degree of change within the system, how long-lasting the reform is and what unexpected consequences there are from the introduction of these changes or reforms. Furthermore, some types of change catalyst are more likely to be successful in inducing change within the system than others. This is not only because some interventions in education systems are more powerful than others but also because their capacity to induce change fits better the change mechanism within the system being reformed.

For example, in a system which has a high level of command structure between the coordinating body and its constituent parts, a policy for change at the classroom level that is underpinned by a strong system of rewards and sanctions is likely to be successful in inducing change at this level. This is in contrast to systems which grant greater degrees of autonomy to their teachers, and consequently the same change mechanism may have less chance of succeeding. Extra-national change agents work in the same way and the OECD's PISA system of international assessment is an example of this. What these globalising bodies are attempting to do is establish a form of global panopticism (cf. Foucault, 1979) where the activities of the various national systems are made visible to a supra-national body, with the consequence that all parts of the system are visible from one single point. However, what this needs is a single surface of comparison or at least a comparative mechanism that can do this, so that enough people have confidence in it for it to be considered useful.

What we have been doing is categorising the system (i.e. a national education system) as a set of institutions and relations between those institutions, or even as a coordinating body for a number of sub-systems, which have a particular relation to the state and a particular position within it. However, this doesn't mean that the state (and, in particular, its boundaries between, and relations with, other parts) and the education system (and its boundaries between, and relations with, other systems) remain the same over time. The shrinking or at least attempted shrinking of the state (from welfarism to neo-liberality in many countries round the world) involves a redefining of what the state is, what an education system is and what the relations between the two are. However, these relations (internally and externally oriented) may change for a number of possible reasons, for example, the invention of new ideas, natural progression, contradictions as historically accumulating structural tensions between open activity systems (cf. Engeström, 2001) and so forth.

It is fairly easy to understand an education system as a coordinating body that directs a number of sub-units, so that if the central authority demands action of a particular type, then these subsidiary bodies will implement its directives. The cohering element in the notion of a system being used here is that one body commands a series of other bodies, though all of them are considered to be elements of a system. However, it is rare for any actual system to function in this way. Within the system the extent and type of power that the coordinating body can exercise over the other elements may be differently exercised. For example, if we consider the Indian education system, one of its characteristics is that there is a large and influential private sector. The private sector educates about 29% of students in the 6–14 age group, and large numbers of its alumni are to be found in powerful professions in society. Thus, a system's coordinating body may have less or more direct relations with different parts of the system. Indeed, it may be that some of these relations become so attenuated that it becomes harder to include them in the system.

Furthermore, systems have internal rules, that is, their elements are arranged in particular ways. Traditional systems have a high degree of specialisation; a clearly defined division of labour; the distribution of official tasks within the organisation; a hierarchical structure of authority with clearly defined areas of responsibility; formal rules which regulate the operation of the organisation; a written administration; a clear separation between what is official and what is personal; and the recruitment of personnel on the basis of ability and technical knowledge. In corporative–clientelist countries, such as India, education systems function with different elements and different relations between them, and these differences are fundamental to the way they work.

Our use of the concept of a system should not be confused with the way it is used within a structural–functionalist framework (cf. Parsons, 1964), which understands society as a complex system whose parts work together to promote solidarity and stability. We are using it here to refer to complicated sets of arrangements that societies make to set in place structures for providing education for children in these societies, and here the notion of a system is not being used to mark out an end point such as stability, stasis, teleology or completeness, but only to refer to those institutional arrangements that all societies make. This doesn't indicate a functionalist perspective; however, what it does suggest is that arrangements of people and resources and allocations of people to functions and roles and the power arrangements that are the backdrop to decision-making are what constitute the system. Again, this doesn't imply that any particular pattern of allocation or arrangement is either the best or even the most popular. What it suggests is that there is a variety of systems and that they work in different ways. Furthermore, those allocations and arrangements change over time.

Another way of thinking about it is as a unified body; coherence lies in its unity. The system is governed not through networks of power (usually one-way) but through its purposes or intentions. Thus, it might consist of a large number of separate entities that have a common purpose. If we look at the history of education systems (and perhaps especially India in the twentieth and twenty-first centuries) the system no longer appears to be coherent or unified, but it still continues to function, or at least seems to be doing so. We are suggesting that the system's conceptual roots are neither political (i.e. they operate through well-established networks of power) nor administrative, but lie with data technology and surveillance (cf. Gough, 1999). What unites the disparate parts of the system is the flows of performance data and their fine-grained analyses from all parts of the system. All the elements of the system – curriculum, policy flows, institutions, bureaucracies, systems of inspection, local authority systems of governance, central government controls, and the like – are now considered to be subservient to the element of data flows. The system coheres and it functions in use through data and is no longer held together by mythologising processes which coalesce round notions of unity, progression and relations (cf. Lawn, 2006).

However, regardless of how we understand the notion of a system (and we have already suggested that we cannot discard the notion altogether), any change to it is always a transformation of the status quo. Therefore, we need to understand how those systems and curricula are currently structured. What this means is that the same programme of reform delivered in different countries is likely to have different effects on the different elements of the system and will have different histories within the system. This has profound implications for models of policy borrowing or, in relation to the principal theme of this book, policy learning.

A Brief History of the Indian Education System

In the first instance we provide an historical perspective on the development of the education system in India, highlighting the changing emphases in government policy. Since independence, the education policies of successive governments have built on the substantial legacies of the Nehruvian period, and these focused on the twin imperatives of plurality and secularism, with a focus on excellence at all levels of the system, and in particular, inclusiveness for all the different types of students. Traditional Hindu education was fundamentally elitist, focusing on the needs of Brahmin families and insisting on Brahmin teachers for their children. During the mogul era, the education system likewise favoured the rich and those children from the higher castes. Though British colonial rule brought with it the idea of a modern state and a modern education system, they also retained the idea that it was the function of the state to train and educate an elite for their future leadership roles. The education system was first developed in the three presidencies (of Bombay, Calcutta and Madras). In the early 1900s, the Indian National Congress called for the formation of a national education system, and in addition they focused on the need for technical and vocational training. In 1920 the Congress Party initiated a boycott of government schools and in their turn founded several national schools and colleges.

Unfortunately, these schools were not a success, as the incentives for graduating with a British education proved to be overwhelming. The British were also keen to recruit to their side a cadre of well-trained bureaucrats to help them run the country. Nehru, however, had a different vision for India, and envisaged it as a secular democracy with a state-led command economy. A comprehensive system of education and massive investment in industrial development were seen as important tools for uniting the country, and especially for healing its divisions, based as these were, and to some extent still are, on wealth, caste and religious differences.

A seminal moment in the history of the Indian education system was the setting up of the Kothari Commission (1964–66), and its principal purpose was to formulate a coherent education policy for India. The commission strongly argued for an education service that was fit for purpose and in particular would develop social and national unity, consolidate democracy, modernise the country and develop social, moral and spiritual values. Its principal recommendation was that a free and compulsory education system for all children up to the age of 14 should be subsequently established. In addition, it argued for the development of teaching languages (Hindi, Sanskrit, regional languages and the three-language formula), equality of educational opportunities (regional, tribal and gender imbalances were to be addressed) and the development and prioritisation of scientific education and research. The commission also emphasised the need to eradicate illiteracy and provide adult education.

In 1986, Rajiv Gandhi, the prime minister at this time, announced a new education policy, the National Policy on Education (NPE), and this was intended to prepare India for the twenty-first century. He argued for the need for change: '(e)ducation in India stands at the crossroads today. Neither normal linear expansion nor the existing pace and nature of improvement can meet the needs of the situation.' The new policy was intended to raise education standards and increase access to education. At the same time, its avowed intention was to safeguard the values of secularism, socialism and equality, which had been promoted since independence.

Despite Nehru's vision of universal education, and the Kothari Commission's recommendation to provide all young children with free and compulsory schooling, in practice a significant proportion of India's young population remained uneducated at the turn of century. Although enrolment in primary education has increased, it is estimated that at least 35 million, and possibly as many as 60 million, children aged 6–14 years currently are not in school, though the situation is getting better. Serious gender, regional and caste disparities still exist. The main problems are the high drop-out rates, low levels of learning and achievement, inadequate school infrastructures, poorly functioning schools, high teacher absenteeism, the large number of teacher vacancies and insufficient funding.

There is still no common school system; instead children are selected for private, government-aided and government schools on the basis of ability to pay and social class or caste. At the top end are English-language schools where students take the prestigious CBSE (Central Board of Secondary Education), CISCE (Council for the Indian Schools Certificates Examination) and IB (International Baccalaureate) examinations, with their globally recognised syllabuses and curricula. Those who cannot afford private schooling attend English-language government-aided schools, where their work is assessed by state-level examination boards. And on the bottom rung are poorly managed government or municipal schools, which cater for the children from the poorest of families. Therefore, even though universal education is safeguarded by the Constitution, and a majority of children go to school, the quality of the education they receive varies widely according to their means and background. In India's 600,000 villages and multiplying urban slum habitats, 'free and compulsory education' is in fact basic literacy instruction dispensed by barely qualified para-teachers.

In the Indian education system national level education policy-making is formulated by the Ministry of Human Resource Development (MHRD), which was established in 1985 through the 174th Amendment to the Government on India Rules. The Ministry comprises the Department of School Education and Literacy and the Department of Higher Education. The former focuses on school education and literacy, which includes elementary, secondary, vocational, adult and teacher education, as well as rights-based education. The latter focuses on universities and post-secondary education, technical education, language education, intellectual property issues and other relevant matters. The development of curriculum, textbooks and pedagogic approaches is the responsibility of the National Council of Educational Research and Training (NCERT), which was set up in 1961. Other important central organisations include the National Council for Teacher Education (NCTE). The NCTE develops and oversees research and training in teacher education. The National University of Educational Planning and Administration (NUEPA) develops research, provides postgraduate training in broad areas of education and social science, and advises the government.

NCERT has been the principal policy instigator in developing the education system. We have already referred to the first national statement on education – the National Policy on Education (NPE) – which was a set of recommendations in 1968 that emanated from the Education Commission (1964–68). The NPE recommended the setting up of a national system of education, which would comprise ten years of general education, followed by two years of senior secondary programmes, and they also suggested that the teacher education curriculum should be rewritten. The drive toward a national system led to the development of a national curriculum framework. The first framework was mapped out in 1975 and new versions were issued in 1988, 2000 and 2005. Each framework focused on different aspects of the system. The 2005 framework, for example, followed these guiding principles (cf. NCERT, 2011): connecting knowledge to life outside school; moving away from rote methods of teaching; enriching the curriculum for the overall development of children beyond the use of textbooks; making examinations flexible and integrating them into classroom life; and nurturing an identity informed by a caring ethos. The framework also addressed the need for system reforms in relation to academic planning and leadership at school levels, examination reforms, and school–community links, including the further involvement of the community in school education. NCERT works with relevant institutions at national, regional and state levels.

The National University of Educational Planning and Administration (NUEPA) is another government body that influences education policy and development at national level. NUEPA was originally set up by UNESCO as the Asian Regional Centre for Educational Planners, Administrators and Supervisors, but later was adopted by the government of India in the late 1960s. The current institute is mandated by the MHRD to foster capacity building and research in the planning and management of the education system. It became officially recognised as a university in 2006 and it now offers postgraduate degree programmes in educational policy, planning and administration.

Teacher training and deployment systems are the responsibility of the National Council for Teacher Education (NCTE), which develops teacher education programme frameworks and standards for qualified teachers to teach in pre-primary, primary, secondary and senior secondary schools. The NCTE monitors and approves institutions that provide teacher education. It has been in existence since 1973 as the advisory body on teacher education to the government and originally it was a part of NCERT. It was finally recognised as a statutory independent body in 1995 under the regulations enshrined in the National Council for Teacher Education Act, 1993 (No. 73 of 1993). NCTE conducts research and training on, and in relation to, teacher education, and plans and coordinates a nationwide teacher education system. Its remit is pre-primary, primary, secondary and senior secondary education, as well as non-formal and adult education.

The National Council for Teacher Education (NCTE) has been responsible for the development of the teacher education framework after India's independence, along with the frameworks for school education. The report of the Education Commission (1964–66) and the National Policy on Education (NPE) in 1986 provided the foundations for current teacher education practices, which include the NPE's proposals for greater teacher professionalism through pre-service and in-service training in the continuum. Their policy projects also include: a greater fit of teacher education to changing contexts, such as an expansion of diversity within the Indian education system; flexible approaches to teacher education to fit local needs; and providing links between theory and practice. The effort to establish a national system of teacher education emerged from a set of recommendations made in the document, *Teacher Education Curriculum:*

A Framework (NCTE, 1978). Its recommendations included: the development of policy and practice that is relevant to the social and personal needs of children and schools; context specificity (such as to rural and urban settings); an interdisciplinary approach; developing a reliable evaluation system; and enhancing research and experimentation practices (ibid.).

Subsequently, the Framework published in 1988 addressed the development of teacher training curricula and the need for teachers to have the skill of effective communication, be able to design and use learning resources, be facilitators for pupils' learning, and actively engage in community life (ibid.). The Framework built on the National Curriculum Framework for Elementary and Secondary School Education of 1988, which promoted learner centred pedagogies and interactive teaching styles. As a further development, the Curriculum Framework for Quality Teacher Education was issued in 1998, reflecting globalisation, privatisation and the impact of technology on education. Pandey (2007) argues that the major changes were in its emphasis on commitment, competence and performance as the guiding principles behind teacher education curricula and programmes. It also addressed the teachers' role in responding to the community, to applying culture-specific pedagogy, and to preparing children to become life-long learners. The Framework identified a separate course structure for different levels and types of education, such as primary, secondary, academic and vocational streams, and education for children with special needs.

The implementation of these frameworks on the ground, however, is quite limited in practice. Many stakeholders are not aware of the framework, and teachers still refer to outdated pedagogic theories originating in the West, neglecting the culture- and context-specific approaches suggested in the new Framework. Critics (such as the World Bank, 1997) suggest that current teacher education approaches do not prepare teachers for handling classes with multigrade students, students with varied learning preparedness, and cultural and linguistic diversity. These issues are expected to increase in importance with the universalisation of elementary education.

The two most recent documents, the *National Curriculum Framework for School Education* (NCERT, 2005) and the *National Curriculum Framework for Teacher Education* (NCTE, 2009), endorse learner-centred approaches, where teachers facilitate learners' active involvement in constructing knowledge, while at the same time taking into consideration the physical, social and cultural contexts of learning. The Framework for Teacher Education highlights the need for enhanced applicability, and a longer duration of the teacher training programme with a larger proportion of school-based training, through which self-study, classroom research, reflection and engagement with other practitioners and activities were to be encouraged. Moreover, the Right to Education Act (RTE) in 2009 advocated equal opportunities, sustainable development, inclusion of the community and the use of information and communication technology (ICT) in education. This reflects a further shift of Indian society towards modernisation.

Regionalisation, Devolution and Decentralisation

One of the key structural axes of the Indian education system is the relationship between the central government and the states. This has implications for one of the most significant recent developments at the global level: the transfer of powers downwards towards the regions. This process, which may involve the creation of new political entities and bodies at more local levels, is known as regionalisation, devolution or decentralisation. Although these words have different meanings in different geographical contexts, they all imply a transfer of authority, responsibility and resources from the national government to lower governmental tiers. In the context of India, this would be at state, regional and local levels.

Among the nation states that had considerable regional autonomy before the onset of globalisation, the trend has also been towards even greater decentralisation. In India, the over-concentration of power in the hands of a few national elites since independence and until the early 1980s brought about a reaction that started a process of redressing the balance from the centre to the regions. In India, state responsibilities embrace public order, police, prisons, irrigation, agriculture and related activities, land, public health, industries other than those centrally assigned, and trade and commerce. In addition, states share, with the central government, authority over economic and social planning, education, labour and forestry. However, this notion of sharing is not quite what it means. It would be misleading to suggest that the central government authority and the states are equal partners and in turn it would be misleading to suggest that the states and the regional and local authorities have equal influence in the development and implementation of policy in the Indian education system. Rather, the lower level bodies have a considerable influence on policies and practices that have been developed at a central level, but that in direct and indirect ways (such as through the use of the central grant system), the central authority can override the assumed equality between the two bodies.

Under the Constitution, responsibility for education is shared between central and state governments. The central government formulates policy, stimulates innovation and develops frameworks. The state governments are responsible for running the education system. This has created problems since states have different resources to allocate to education, and it is the inadequacy of resources that has recently become the most pressing and central issue. Allocation is another issue, and in general richer, southern states do better than the poorer, northern ones.

Successive governments of the 1990s set up systems to decentralise decision-making autonomies to the states and regions. Since then, the government has set up three tiers of autonomous units of local government called the Panchayat Raj Institutions (PRI). The system currently comprises over 600 districts, 6600 blocks and 250,000 Gram Panchayats (village councils) across the country. Each body has elected representatives who make decisions on education matters in their area. Government bodies, such as the MHRD, NCERT, NCTE and NUEPA, work with these units to involve schools, communities and individuals in their decision making and implementation of schemes and initiatives. The levels of devolved autonomy vary among states, regions and localities, and, in addition, there is some uncertainty about the actual level of autonomy and effectiveness of the Panchayat Raj Institutions.

Recent Reform Initiatives – Sarva Shiksha Abhiyan

Sarva Shiksha Abhiyan (SSA), translated as the *Education for All Movement*, is a programme established by the government of India in 2000 with the aim of achieving universal access to elementary education. The programme was set up to provide for a variety of interventions for universal access and retention, the bridging of gender and social category gaps in elementary education and improving the quality of learning. Working in partnership with state governments, SSA interventions include the opening of new schools and alternative schooling facilities, the rebuilding of schools and the construction of additional classrooms, toilets and provision for drinking water, provisioning for teachers, regular in-service training for teachers and academic resource support, free textbooks and uniforms and support for improving learning achievement outcomes. Improving the education of life skills for children with special needs and providing access to technology-mediated learning were also targeted.

The curricular and structural changes demanded by the SSA were guided by the notion of an holistic view of education, as repeatedly referred to in the *National Curriculum Framework* (NCERT, 2005), with implications for a systemic restructuring of the entire content and process of education and in particular, for the curriculum, teacher education, educational planning and management. SSA above all prioritises the notion of equity, in its original mission statement and in its subsequent restructuring, and here it is referring to not only equal opportunities, but also the creation of conditions in which the disadvantaged sections of the society, children of scheduled castes (SC), scheduled tribes (ST), other backward classes such as Muslim minorities, landless agricultural workers and children with special needs, etc., were to be provided with genuine opportunities in life. Access implies an understanding of the educational needs and predicaments of these traditionally excluded categories. A concern with gendered issues implies not only an effort to enable girls to keep up with boys but also to view education in the perspective spelt out in the National Policy on Education 1986/92, for example, a decisive intervention to bring about a basic change in the status of women. It also implies that the teacher is and should be central, to motivate, to innovate and to create a culture in the classroom, and beyond the classroom, that might produce an inclusive environment for children, especially for girls from oppressed and marginalised backgrounds.

Currently the Sarva Shiksha Abhiyan (SSA) is implemented as a centrally sponsored scheme in partnership with state governments for universalising elementary education across the country. Over the years there has been a significant spatial and numerical expansion of elementary schools in the country. Access and enrolment at the primary stage of education have reached near universal levels. The number of out-of-school children has reduced significantly. The gender gap in elementary education has narrowed and the percentage of children belonging to scheduled castes and tribes enrolled is proportionate to their population. Yet, the goal of universal elementary education continues to elude India. There remains an unfinished agenda of universal education at the upper primary stage. The number of children, particularly children from disadvantaged groups and weaker sections, who drop out of school before completing upper primary education, remains high. The quality of learning is not always entirely satisfactory even in the case of children who complete elementary education.

In 2009, the Right to Education (RTE) Act was passed and it was incorporated into the SSA approaches, strategies and norms (MHRD, 2015). The RTE Act, formally the Right of Children to Free and Compulsory Education Act, was developed as the 86th amendment to the Constitution of India, and came into force in 2010. Article 21A and the Right to Education Act (RTE) was passed by the parliament of India on the 1 April 2013. The title of the RTE Act incorporates the words 'free and compulsory'. 'Free education' means that no child, other than a child who has been admitted by his or her parents to a school which is not supported by the appropriate government, should be liable to pay any kind of fee or charges or expenses which may prevent him or her from pursuing and completing elementary education. 'Compulsory education' is an obligation on the appropriate state and local authorities to provide and ensure admission, attendance and completion of elementary education by all children in the 6–14 age group. With this, India moved forwards to a rights-based framework that gives to the central and state governments a legal obligation to implement this fundamental child right as enshrined in the Article 21A of the Constitution, in accordance with the provisions of the RTE Act.

The Act specifies the duties and responsibilities of appropriate state governments, local authorities and parents in providing free and compulsory education, and sharing financial and other responsibilities between the central and state governments. It lays down the norms and standards relating, amongst others, to pupil–teacher ratios (PTRs), buildings and infrastructure, school-working days and teacher-working hours. It provides for the rational deployment of teachers by ensuring that the specified pupil–teacher ratio is maintained for each school, rather than just as an average for the state or district or block, thus ensuring that there is no urban–rural imbalance in teacher postings. It also provides for the prohibition of the deployment of teachers for non-educational work, other than the decennial census, elections to local authority, state legislatures and parliament, and disaster relief.

It provides for the appointment of appropriately trained teachers, i.e. teachers with the requisite entry and academic qualifications. It prohibits physical punishment and mental harassment; screening procedures for the admission of children; capitation fees; and private tuition by teachers and schools without recognition. It provides for the development of a curriculum to fit the values enshrined in the Constitution, and which would ensure the all-round development of the child, building on the child's knowledge, potentiality and talent and allowing the child to be free of fear, trauma and anxiety through a system of child friendly and child centred learning experiences.

The changes incorporated in the SSA approach, reflecting the RTE Act, were not merely confined to norms for teachers or classrooms, but encompassed a vision and approach to elementary education, as evidenced in the shift to child entitlements and quality elementary education in regular schools. Under SSA, most states have included a variety of interventions for quality improvement. These include pilot programmes within the Learning Enhancement Programme (LEP) such as teacher training, material development and specific subject-oriented programmes.

However, in practice, the states and the regions have found it difficult to implement the various components of the Act. Rural schools in particular faced difficulties in, for example, providing the infrastructure and teachers to support children with disabilities, enforcing the qualification rules for teachers, reducing pupil–teacher ratios, and enrolling children in 'age appropriate' classes. According to the RTE norms and standards, the teacher–pupil ratio should be 1:30, though schools often have class sizes as large as 70. Supporting teachers to handle students with low learning preparedness, often seen among first-generation learners, also created difficulties. Currently, about 6–7% of primary children are seen to repeat grades and about 3% drop out. Grade repetition tends to be higher in rural areas, such as 16% in West Bengal and Jharkhand in 2009–10.

It has been five years since the RTE has taken effect, and many schools are expected to have achieved the mandated conditions. The recent Annual Status of Education Report (ASER) shows that there are only about 50% of government schools complying with the pupil–teacher ratio norms, about 75% with drinking water norms, 65% with usable toilet facilities requirements, and 20% have computers. In terms of learning outcomes, less than half of grade five students were found to be able to read texts for grade two level and only about 20% of grade two students were able to count up to nine (ASER, 2015). Perpetuating absenteeism and expanding private schooling also suggest that the quality of basic education, especially in government schools, is still far from desirable (Pritchett and Pandey, 2006).

There is a tendency for the system and the school curriculum to ignore the ground realities of children, and to espouse deficit theories of learning, which assume unjustifiably that children from disadvantaged backgrounds are also lacking in ability or interest. For example, the child may speak a different language at home, may be a first generation school attender and may continue to help with domestic chores of the family, but the design and transaction of the curriculum fails to recognise this and build on it. It is common for the system to claim that children who come to school at an older age of say eight or nine years 'know nothing', just because they do not know how to read and write. This again is a failure of the system to recognise that children are natural learners and that they bring with them sophisticated structures of learning and constructing knowledge. Any attempt to improve the quality of education, SSA claimed, would succeed only if it went hand in hand with steps to promote equality and social justice. This can only be achieved when the knowledge and experience of children from all backgrounds and particularly those from disadvantaged groups are foregrounded in school learning with primacy given to their socio-cultural context.

The education system has adopted a subject-based approach to the organisation of the curriculum, focusing on areas that readily lend themselves to being formulated as subjects. These subject boundaries have become rigid, are determined more by the disciplines they are associated with at higher stages of learning, and have little connection with how children actually develop their conceptual understanding. Moreover, areas that do not lend themselves to being organised in textbooks, for example visual and performing arts or work education, are relegated to extra or co-curricular activities. Any new concern or problem, such as environmental awareness, human rights, value education or disaster management, is addressed piecemeal or as an add-on, without incorporating it cohesively into the curriculum.

There is an emphasis on the reproduction of 'information' learnt by rote methods, rather than on 'constructing knowledge' from experience. The schools usually 'transmit information' through lessons 'delivered', where children are expected to passively listen, write or respond to tasks on an individual basis. And, as with curricula round the world, curriculum standards and pedagogical approaches are conflated, and priority is given to assessment-driven and external accountability education mechanisms.

The Indian education system, as with any education system, is composed of parts, relations between those parts and relations between the parts and the central coordinating body. These particular parts and relations have an effect on the history and flow of any intervention in that system. For example, the particular relations between the central coordinating body, the government of India, and the Indian states, though complicated and at times subject to negotiation, is a crucial factor in how the Indian system is and can be reformed. It is clear that policy processes are central to the model of policy learning that we are arguing for in this book and it is this issue that we address in the next chapter.

3

THE SPREAD OF IDEAS

The recipient country of the policy borrowing process that concerns us then is India, with its massive education system, devolved governance to the states, and large private sector, largely populated by children of the burgeoning middle classes. India wanted to learn from other national systems, and in this book we are concerned with these policy-borrowing or policy-learning processes, both at a theoretical level and in relation to an actual instance of such a process. In this chapter we examine the spread of ideas from one environment to another, and it would be naïve of us to accept the narrative that this is an uncomplicated and straightforward process. We have already suggested that curriculum reform and policy-making is a complex and contested enterprise. And as has been already observed, policy ideas are an object of contest and struggle between competing ideologies, education visions, personal interests and political or organisational positions. All of these forces come together in an incubator of international, national and local contexts. Thus, how ideas move between and have traction in different environments is a key part of the argument we are making here.

Two Stories

1. Teaching as a social enterprise

In 1989, an undergraduate in the Woodrow Wilson School of Public Policy at Princeton University submitted her sociology thesis under the title 'An Argument and Plan for the Creation of the Teacher Corps'. Wendy Kopp (1989) set out a plan for a cadre of teacher candidates, on the model of the 1960s' 'Peace Corps', to be deployed in socially challenging urban schools across America in order to raise standards of educational performance. Kopp's thesis combined four elements: a critique of standard models for the delivery of teacher education and teachers; what she saw as a widespread desire on the part of new graduates to undertake socially worthwhile work for at least a short period of time; the mobilisation of philanthropic funding to sustain novel approaches; and a centralised organisation to manage recruitment, development and deployment. Somewhat unusually for new graduates, Kopp followed up her undergraduate work: she set about fundraising, and raised half a million dollars from philanthropists for her new organisation, Teach for America. She began active recruitment on a national scale, making use of extensive publicity, and a highly selective application process. Kopp's scheme requiring a short initial time commitment to teaching, assessed and deployed new teacher candidates through centralised application, training and placement processes. Her expressed mission was to attract 'top graduates' from the most highly selective universities into teaching. The first 500 Teach for America graduates entered teaching in 1990. Teach for America reported a budget of $212 million 20 years later and a staff of 1400, and Kopp herself was paid over $400,000 a year (TFA, 2015).

In the late 1990s, concerns about teacher supply and perceptions of teacher quality in London schools led the business lobby group London First to commission a piece of work from McKinsey and Co (Wigdortz, 2012) on possible strategies to address what appeared to be a deepening recruitment crisis. In 2001, Brett Wigdortz, then a McKinsey staffer who had worked on the London report, left his employer and established a new organisation in London, strongly modelled on Kopp's work. Teach First adopted similar principles: philanthropic funding, a selective application process, extensive marketing and a strongly worded mission couched in the language of social justice in order to break the link between socio-economic status and educational outcomes. Teach for America had, essentially, crossed the Atlantic. Over the next decade, Kopp's model was widely copied, extending to countries as far apart and as different as Estonia (2006), India (2007), Chile (2007), Australia (2008), Germany (2008), China (2008), Malaysia (2010), Bulgaria (2011) and Bangladesh (2012). The global Teach for All organisation emerged: all national member organisations recruit and train young teachers who set out to both influence students in the short-term and go on to create system change in various sectors as alumni, whether they stay teaching in schools or not. As it has spread, however, Teach for All has adapted itself to local circumstances. In the United States, Teach for America by-passed conventional university-based providers of teacher education entirely; in England and Australia, the local organisations chose to commission their training from university teacher education departments. In the United States, Teach for America was substantially philanthropically funded; in England, Teach First draws on a mix of philanthropic and government funding, as it does in Australia. The model and conception is widespread; its local applications are distinctive.

2. Taking education assessment global

The Organisation for European Economic Cooperation (OEEC) was established in 1948, essentially to manage the US-financed Marshall Plan to reconstruct

Europe after the Second World War, and it was one of the institutions, along with the European Coal and Steel Community, and later the European Economic Community, which led to the re-establishment of open, market economies in Europe. As the EEC took on the task of leading European cooperation, the OEEC needed a new role, and became the Organisation for Economic Cooperation and Development (OECD) in 1961. Other countries – the USA, Canada and Japan were the first – joined; in the early twenty-first century, the OECD had 34 members, accounting for something like 80% of the world's trade. As early as 1964, member states wanted comparative statistics on education in order to try to compare skill levels of students between and within national educational systems in order to forecast labour markets. But the OECD considered the data available to be flimsy, and for much of its first 40 years it was a free trade forum.

Change came in the 1980s. The Reagan administration established a national commission to study the American education system; their 1983 report, *A Nation at Risk* (National Commission on Excellence in Education, 1983), produced disappointing results: 23 million adults and 17% of juveniles were functionally illiterate. Ronald Reagan made school reform a priority of his administration; poor educational performance was a national security risk, and the American administration looked to ways to generate internationally comparable statistical data which would help to drive its pressure for change. The American administration looked to the OECD to develop indicators. The OECD Education Directorate was sceptical. Recalling the 1964 experience, it did not believe that education could be compared through statistics and comparative tables. But the United States gained unexpected support from France. Jean-Pierre Chevènement, socialist minister of education, believed that comparative data would highlight the failings of the elitist French educational system, and in the later 1980s, the Americans and French persuaded the OECD to develop a new set of comparative education statistics (Martens and Liebfried, 2008). The first *Education at a Glance* (OECD, 1992) data was published in 1992, but it was limited to comparative administrative data; what was needed was a mechanism to compare measures of performance. When Tom Alexander, head of the Directorate for Education, proposed a testing programme to member states, however, most of them were opposed, seeing it as foreign interference in home affairs (Martens and Liebfried, 2008). It took intensive lobbying before the Programme for International Student Assessment (PISA) was agreed in 1997; the OECD then recruited a large staff to design, what they imagined to be, a methodologically sound testing regime. The first PISA tests were run in 2000, and the results published in 2001.

What embedded PISA in global policy debates were the first PISA results for Germany. Germany had always believed in the excellence of its education system, but its students performed poorly in PISA 2000; 'PISA shock' had a profound effect in Germany, but the effect on the OECD was perhaps even greater. The test had revealed, so it seemed, something that had hitherto been unclear, and no government could now take the risk of not using PISA. The second PISA tests ran in 2003 with more countries participating, and then more joined again in each of the next runs of the tests, in 2006 (by which time Germany after internal reforms was performing much better), 2009, 2012 and 2015. In 2015, countries accounting for more than 85% of the world economy were in PISA. Around the world, policies are now designed as a response to PISA performance, and what the tests appeared to show. Finland, hitherto a small north European backwater of education policy attracted global attention for its high PISA performance. The OECD teams added country surveys and policy advice to their portfolio and in early 2015 published a global analysis of the characteristics of more and less effective education policy initiatives (OECD, 2015).

India dipped its toes in the PISA waters and then withdrew. Of the 74 countries tested in the PISA 2009 cycle, two Indian states (Himachal Pradesh and Tamil Nadu) were placed in 72nd and 73rd position out of 74 countries that participated in both reading and mathematics, and 73rd and 74th position in science. The poor results in PISA were greeted with dismay in the Indian media. India withdrew from the next round of PISA testing, in August 2012, with the Indian government attributing its actions to the unfairness of this testing process for Indian learners. The *Indian Express* (9 March 2012) reported that:

> (t)he ministry (of education) has concluded that there was a socio-cultural disconnect between the questions and Indian students. The ministry will write to the OECD and drive home the need to factor in India's 'socio-cultural milieu'. India's participation in the next PISA cycle will hinge on this.

In June 2013, the Indian government, still concerned with the future prospect of fairness of PISA testing relating to Indian students, again withdrew from the 2015 round of PISA testing.

Changing Practices in Reform

These then are two instances of the spread of ideas and their conversion into educational practices: Teach for All and PISA. Each story is distinctive, but they share a common feature. They are ideas that have transformed policy, and practices, around the world, exerting influence over politicians and policy-makers, researchers and practitioners, education leaders and teachers. There may be some doubt as to whether Teach for All and PISA reflect neatly what generally happens. However, they ask questions which are at the core of our preoccupations: how do ideas travel in education, and how can we make them travel more effectively?

We can answer these questions in a number of ways. The first of these would be to explore the nature and characteristics of the phenomena themselves. Teach for All and PISA share some common features. Both are relatively recent.

Both have developed extremely rapidly. Both have extended their influence widely. Both have local variants and detractors. Both operate in a space of policy borrowing and replication: an idea developed, copied and transplanted, in different contexts and settings from that in which they were originally devised. At the more abstract level, both Teach for All and PISA have been presented as exemplifying complex, globalising transformations in policy thinking over the last generation, associated with the triumph of neo-liberalism. Both are consistent with government impatience with traditional formal structures. Each operates in a policy context which draws on some common features: a preoccupation with the attainment, achievement and skill levels of individuals, a focus on testing to assess not simply the performance of individuals but the overall effectiveness of educational institutions and systems, a focus on the discourse of 'equity' as a component of effectiveness, and an impatience with well-established public structures in education. Teach for All, and its many local forms, grew out of a frustration with the perceived ineffectiveness of traditional approaches to teacher education and development, replacing institutionally focused approaches to teacher education with a focus on the individual teacher whose agency can, through commitment, drive and determination, overcome the constraints of social and economic structures. The promise of the UK version, Teach First, is to break the link between low attainment and deprivation (Wigdortz, 2012). The underlying argument that deprivation is not destiny is highly consistent with the atomised neo-liberal view of the individual as a self-determining agent. In the same way, PISA is a challenge to governments, requiring them to look hard at their formal educational structures, structures shaped by institutional practices and to ask hard questions about the effectiveness of those systems in equipping individuals with the skills needed for the developing labour market, although it should be said that elsewhere the OECD has developed a strong focus on other dimensions of educational effectiveness including issues of civic and democratic engagement. Both Teach for All and PISA are predominantly concerned with the impact of educational practices and interventions; the concern is with outcomes, and the implied argument is that experimentation that drives improvement in skills for individuals is to be prized.

But to characterise these two instances in this way goes only so far. The issue is not about the characteristics of Teach for All and PISA, but about why they have been so influential and why they have travelled so well. Pasi Sahlberg (2011a), writing from the relatively comfortable perspective which comes from having been a leading policy-maker in Finland – one of the most consistently successful of PISA performers – has pointed to the influence of what he calls GERM – the Global Education Reform Movement. Sahlberg (2011b) argues that GERM after the 1980s has increasingly become adopted as an educational reform orthodoxy within many education systems throughout the world, now promoted through international development agencies and private enterprises.

Sahlberg (2011b) identifies five features of GERM. The first is a preoccupation with standardisation through outcomes-based education reform, focusing attention on educational outcomes assessed by external testing and evaluation. Standardisation depends on centrally prescribed curricula, with detailed performance targets, frequent testing of students and teachers, and test-based accountability, and has produced, he argues, an increasing homogenisation of education policies worldwide. The second common feature of GERM is a focus on core subjects in schools, particularly literacy and numeracy, and science. Basic student knowledge and skills in reading, writing and mathematics are seen as prime targets and indices of education reforms at the expense of the arts, music and physical education.

The third characteristic of GERM is the search for lower-risk ways to meet prescribed learning outcomes, narrowing teaching and learning to focus on what Sahlberg calls 'guaranteed content' to meet test requirements. The fourth characteristic of *GERM* is the use of corporate management models to drive reform and improvement, rather than the moral goals of human development. As a result national policy development and the enhancement of an education system's own capabilities to develop are ranked below its capacity to learn from apparently effective practices in other systems; internal development comes to matter less than policy borrowing. The final characteristic cited by Sahlberg is the widespread adoption of test-based accountability so that school performance, especially raising student achievement, is closely tied to 'processes of accrediting, promoting, inspecting, and ultimately, rewarding or punishing schools and teachers'.

Seen in this way, we have an explanation as to why Teach for All and PISA have travelled so effectively and been adopted so widely; they are consistent with the over-arching paradigm for education reform which has swept the world since the 1980s. This is a radically different explanation from that which is normally offered in policy and practice circles. There, the arguments of politicians, policy-makers and practitioners are mostly around the 'superiority' of the models, the effectiveness of their practices and the extent to which they offer tools for the effective implementation of underlying policy challenges: the recruitment of teachers, particularly in hard-to-staff schools, the evaluation of educational effectiveness, and the comparative performance of education institutions. Sahlberg's (2011b) account of the Global Education Reform Movement offers a shift in perspective; Teach for All and PISA have travelled well not simply because of their intrinsic qualities but because they are hugely consistent with over-arching assumptions about what makes for a good idea.

Set in an historical context, we cannot explain patterns of policy influence and policy borrowing without referring to wider paradigms. There may be no direct read-off, but in structural terms, both Teach for All and PISA reflect changing assumptions about how practice is enacted *in the light of* changing assumptions about explanatory ideas. They cannot be seen, or understood, separately from massive shifts in global social and economic policies over the last 40 years. Since the oil shock of the 1970s, governments around the world have been wrestling with questions of how to afford, and evaluate, the effectiveness of public services. The generally optimistic, though no less ideologically imbued, belief in the capacity of governments and agencies to accelerate social and economic development through government-led action have fallen apart. On this view, not directly, but indirectly, the oil-price shock begets neo-liberalism, which begets the Global Education Reform Movement, which begets Teach for All and PISA.

How Education Ideas Travel

Our focus here is not specifically about Teach for All, nor about PISA. It is, instead, about the reasons for one nation's failure to bring often excellent proposals for reform and improvement to fruition, and the lessons which can be learnt from that for the effective improvement of educational practices more generally. Our focus is and has been on education reform in India, though paradoxically this is not of primary importance in our study. It is a study of policy implementation and policy borrowing, and the frustrations of reform. We are clear that it is a study of both context and policy ideas. As we completed our work, we were aware of two equally powerful ideas: first, that Indian education, Indian educational administrators and Indian educational reformers were operating in a context which was defined by India's own history, experiences, society, rapidly changing economy, administrative systems and governmental practices, but also, secondly that they were operating in a context in which international policy exchange was highly prized. Indian education reform was both Indian and education reform, located in the complex, often overwhelming realities of India and in the equally complex arena of international policy exchange. We have attempted to tease out that inter-relationship of ideas about education reform. If we are ultimately pessimistic about the ability of any system simply to implement borrowed policies, we are also clear that in a globalised education reform context, the attempt to link the national and the global is essential to effective improvement.

We began by noting that India has been particularly, and increasingly, open to the suggestions and urgings of international organisations as to how to improve educational performance; it operated in an open market for ideas about change and development, and has managed increasingly complex relationships between local and central government, between public and private provision and between government and non-governmental actors. Put differently, ideas have travelled, and have travelled freely between different parts of the Indian education system. But those ideas have not been successful, by which we mean that the achievements of reform have fallen a long way short of the expectations and aspirations of reformers. Too many reform initiatives have foundered. Explanations for this dichotomy between openness to reform and dialogue and ineffectiveness of outcomes are at the core of the argument we are making. It involves considering several interlocking ideas. One is about the nature, forms and extent of the ideas that have been implemented, that is, the nature of the policies and practices that have travelled, and the details of the policies that have been implemented. This involves looking both at global education reform ideas, two of which we have just examined, and at the deep-rooted ideas about education, schooling, the role of teachers, the nature of learning and the nature of childhood which are characteristic of India. Substance matters and the specifics of ideas matter. Put differently, ideas are not merely ciphers.

A second theme is about the processes by which ideas and policies have travelled; the dissemination processes, through books, conferences, meetings, projects that have sought to put these ideas for reform into practice. These processes operate in interlocking circles: the circles of academic research and evidence about policy development and implementation, and the circles of administrative networks inside and outside India. The relationship between the substance of ideas and the processes by which they are disseminated is not constant. Teach for India is a local manifestation of Teach for All, but the process by which it was developed is quite different from the ways in which ideas about educational inclusion and education for all children were communicated and disseminated. These examples could be multiplied.

Another theme is about the process of implementation, about the details by which ideas are translated into policy and regulations, about systems of administration that are vital to the success of implementing reforms, about the politics of relationships between central and local administrations, and about the budgetary and managerial details of administration. Our concerns are both about the ways in which the interplay between the substance of reform ideas, the processes of policy lending and borrowing, and the details of implementation interact, and the implications of these not just for outcomes in India but more generally for policy borrowing and policy learning.

Ideas travel. Good ideas travel, and so do bad ideas. The ways in which ideas travel, and the ways in which they might travel better, has attracted considerable recent attention. As Mary Morgan (2010: 7) observes,

> while it is tempting to imagine that there is a free market in facts and that good facts will somehow travel freely of their own accord, maybe, just as 'bad money drives out good money', bad facts (poorly attested, dubious, fictional) can drive good (well evidenced) facts out of circulation. [....] many facts do travel well, retaining their integrity when they do so, for we all regularly transfer and make use of facts – without subverting them – in new contexts, often without even noticing that we are doing so.

One of our preoccupations in this chapter is the ways in which ideas and facts travel and how those with an interest in their doing so can help them travel better. This also involves consideration of several linked factors.

In her study of 'how facts travel', Mary Morgan (2010) focused on the characteristics of facts [or ideas] that led them to travel well or not, isolating two over-riding factors. First, 'that facts travel well when they travel with integrity; and secondly, that facts travel well when they travel fruitfully'. 'Travelling well' captures the idea that the content, or substance, of an idea is maintained more or less 'intact' during its travel, that it is, at the end (or, indeed, during) its journey, as recognisable as the idea it was when it began. This turns out to be extremely difficult for ideas in education, where local practices, and indeed local languages, can shift the meaning of ideas beyond their original conception. Ideas about 'inclusive education' are a case in point: just what 'inclusion' means, and who is 'included' turns out, as we will see, to be a complex matter, so that, eventually, the practices of inclusion may mean different things at different stages of the journey from conceptualisation to implementation. 'Travelling fruitful' is different, and in some apparent tension with facts, as Mary Morgan (2010: 8) observes: 'they find new uses, gain new functions, coalesce in new patterns and make new narratives'. This directs attention to the ways in which users deploy facts and ideas in different contexts. The complementarity between the integrity of ideas and their utility in new contexts is an important key to understanding the processes of reform and implementation. Sahlberg's (2011a) account of GERM is a coherent account of a set of policy assumptions that have travelled with integrity because of their fruitfulness in the light of the over-arching paradigm for education change, itself a product of large-scale assumptions about economy and society.

But this takes us only so far. Not all ideas translate simply, and if they did then the arguments about the interlocking importance of ideas, translation and implementation would have less force. Innovation practices matter as much as the translation of ideas. Studies of innovation and diffusion have broadened in recent years, so that a concern with the integrity and fruitfulness of the ideas themselves needs to be set aside from parallel work on the translation of ideas globally. Studies of innovation have historically made two assumptions. As Rogers (2003) puts it, we assume that little re-invention of the innovation takes place as it diffuses; and we assume it retains its integrity, and, moreover, diffusion channels shift the innovation from actor to actor. It turns out that both these assumptions are misplaced. Czarniawska and Sevon (2005) have drawn together a series of studies of how ideas, learning objects and practices travel in the global economy, which shift radically assumptions about how ideas travel. In place of the assumption of invariant diffusion through diffusion channels, Czarniawska and Sevon (2005) argue that innovations undergo processes of translation when one social actor adopts another's use of an innovation, and the translation process modifies both the imitated and the imitator. The same innovation does not influence passive adopters. Social agents actively translate what travels to them in order to meet their own needs in their own location at a particular time. Invariant innovation is a misplaced assumption; what is translated differs from its translation because actors transform what travels to fit their unique needs in their specific local settings.

Taken together, Morgan's (2010) focus on integrity and fruitfulness and Czarniawska and Sevon's (2005) ideas on transformation provide a useful conceptual lens through which to contextualise these processes. We are concerned both with the ideas that are being explored, exchanged and implemented, and with the adoption process that transformed them and those implementing them.

In short, in trying to understand how interventions in education systems work and ideas travel, in the first instance we need to remind ourselves of the principal elements of a public educational practice, namely, that it comprises the state's deployment of human resources, its strategic hold over infrastructure and other material and financial resources, its mobilisation of ceremonies, rituals, meanings and values, and its creation and maintenance of a central value system. Change to an education system is always a change to the status quo; to what already exists. Therefore, in trying to understand how national education systems, and their curricula, change in response to external initiatives and practices, we need to understand how those systems and curricula are currently structured. What this means is that the same set of ideas developed in different countries is likely to have different effects on the different elements of the system and will have different histories within the system. The next chapter provides a case study of one of these productive practices and plots the way a set of ideas about teacher training was transported from one country to our recipient country, India.

4

Teachers as Professional Learners

In this chapter we examine the issue of teacher training, both pre- and in-service, and explore attempts to institute reforms of these important matters within the national context that concerns us, the Indian education system. This means that any model of teacher learning environments that we might devise inevitably has to confront, and respond to, current arrangements and understandings of them. For example, the degree to which teacher training institutes in India have autonomy over their own curricula or the extent and type of in-service provision within the states are significant factors in the implementation of the model we argue for here.

We are concerned then, with productive learning environments and how we can construct these within the constraints and enablements of the teacher training system in India. Inevitably we are engaged in making judgements about a number of issues, such as the pedagogic mode (the type of relationship between the teacher-trainer and the student teachers), the learning mode (the type of learning approach that underpins the work of the teacher-trainer), the resources and technologies needed to allow that learning to take place, formative feedback mechanisms by the teacher-trainer (the modes, approaches and purposes), where the learning environment is, timings of different activities during the teaching sessions, the tasks that the student-teachers are expected to complete, formative learning approaches (including assessment for learning approaches), and how the learning can be transferred to other environments. Learners here are student teachers and teachers already in service, and their learning environments are university and higher education institutions, schools and in-service training institutes in India.

Models of Teacher Training

There are perhaps three dominant models of teaching: craft knowledge, executive technician and professional learner, and we consider each of them before giving reasons for preferring the latter. Models are representations of the real world, without the extraneous detail. They are not the real world and it would be a mistake to think that they are. They are designed to help us better understand how the world works. However, their use raises a number of questions: for example, what representational purpose do they have? What kinds of entity are they? What is their pedagogic function? In addition, any model that we articulate has normative elements; that is, we are explicitly suggesting that this model is better than other models that could be devised.

There are four ways of distinguishing between different models and judging that one is better than another. The first is epistemic: a model is superior to another because it is more empirically adequate. The second is the converse, so that a version of reality is better than another because it contains fewer contradictions, disjunctions and aporias. A third approach focuses on the giving of reasons, and concludes that some reasons and systems of rationality are superior to others, and therefore should be preferred. A fourth approach is pragmatic in a philosophical sense: a model is better than another because it is more practically adequate or referenced to/part of extant frameworks of meaning. The productive learning model that we favour is more coherent, more empirically adequate, better referenced to frameworks of meaning, and is underpinned by a more apt rationale than other models.

Craft knowledge

Craft knowledge has the following characteristics. It is rooted in practice and in the routines that shape practice, and this rules out certain types of learning or pedagogic approaches. This means that imitation and scaffolding various attempts to perform the activities are key to the development of this type of knowledge. The teacher or facilitator is the expert practitioner and knowledge is derived from exposure to the performances of the expert. The expert is therefore not primarily a skilled pedagogue but a skilled practitioner. The emphasis is placed on observing and imitating the practice. The justification for this is that the nature of the practice is better understood in these terms, that is, the learning object – becoming and being a good teacher – is a craft activity.

Craft knowledge values situated understanding and downplays the importance of technical know-how and critical reflection. This leaves little room for what might be called research-based knowledge, even if this is understood in a non-technicist way and as having a non-binding quality to it. Though advocates of craft-based knowledge accept that there may be a role for systematic propositional knowledge, this is confined to what is taught, or subject-based knowledge, rather than to the processes of teaching and learning that the teacher or student teacher is engaged in. Furthermore, this entails a clear separation between content and process knowledge or between the learning object and the pedagogic process. In addition, this focus on practical judgements as the essence of the teaching activity fails to account for ethical and epistemological elements in the judgements teachers make. These judgements as a consequence of their lack of reflective critique and adherence to external expert judgement may be inherently conservative and potentially unreliable, based as they are on observations of existing practice and common popularisations.

Executive technician

The second of our teaching models is the executive technician. This requires the teacher to perform in a particular way; to have, and be able to execute, a repertoire of pre-conceived actions. In this model, teaching is a rule-based activity and learning is understood as the assimilation of these rules and ways of enacting them, without recourse to critical reflection or situated understanding. The executive technician model (cf. Winch, 2014) recognises the value of research findings, and this means that it is not thought appropriate for teachers to interpret those findings for themselves. Educational researchers generate findings which can be expressed as protocols for action, and the role of the teacher is to implement these protocols in the most efficient way possible given that there are always situational constraints. One consequence of this is that the knowledge which is being transferred tends to lack a sense of change, emergence, immediacy or relevance. This positions the learning object, these rules and protocols, outside space and time and effectively reifies it. This also applies to the assimilative and performative functions of learning.

These rules are identified by researchers and practical policy-makers as external to the setting. They are not situation-specific or even sensitive to the particularities of the setting in which they are being applied. Educational research is understood as the making of nomothetic statements about educational activities; educational disputes about how teachers should behave in the classroom are settled by a-theoretical and value-free empirical enquiry; and theoretical knowledge of educational matters is thought of as superior to practical knowledge, with the result that practice is understood as the efficient application of theoretical knowledge constructed by professional experts. Learning at pre-service and in-service levels then is reduced to the assimilation of these rules and to ways of following them in concrete situations such as classrooms. A more refined version of the executive technician model is that educational propositional knowledge should not be understood as being applicable in every possible circumstance and as having a certainty of outcome, but it can act as a guide to practical action. This brings back a measure of interpretative activity into the proceedings.

Professional learning

Both the craft and executive technician models can be contrasted with a professional learning model. Professional learning emanates and is derived from an understanding of the characteristics and functions of being a classroom teacher in the context of where that teaching takes place, in our case, India. Apart from the content and methodological knowledge that teachers need in order to plan and teach a lesson, they also have to take a variety of other factors into consideration and integrate them in a coherent, efficient and pedagogically effective way. Among these are the previous knowledge, schooling biographies and expectations of their students, the individual differences between them (e.g. capabilities, interests and motivations), the objectives of the programme and the overall institution, as well as their own pedagogical aims, theoretical assumptions and values. Teachers have to make a considerable number of instantaneous and ad hoc decisions; they need to react to and take the lead in classroom interactions and modify their plans and methodological procedures according to the needs of students at specific points in time during the lesson. Ideally they should create an atmosphere that encourages learning and communication and make sure that the task level is neither too high nor too low. In addition to this, institutions as well as classes have their own particular norms and patterns of interaction and communication. Teachers play a key role in mediating between this institutional culture and their students. They usually determine the content of classroom talk, organise the distinct phases of the lesson, determine the behaviour that is expected from students, select who is permitted to respond to a question or contribute to a discussion, decide what kind of answers are regarded as valid, and so forth.

The fact that teachers have to take a multitude of sequential and simultaneous decisions which have to take account of personal, interpersonal, interactive, disciplinary, pedagogic and institutional factors requires a new approach to in-service teacher training and development. Imposing a pre-defined and fixed innovation on teachers (and students) in diverse institutional and regional contexts in a coercive, top-down fashion is counter-productive and likely to make them revert to 'safe' routinised practices. It seems more promising to encourage practitioners to try out new ideas in their classroom, to make adjustments and then justify their decisions. To this end an awareness of the contexts teachers work in and their own behavioural and communicative patterns is developed. Participants analyse their own classes, strengthen their communicative competences and classroom management strategies, and amplify their pool of teaching resources.

Donald Schon focused, in his seminal work *The Reflective Practitioner* (2005), specifically on how practitioners operate and learn in workplace settings. He suggested that most of our knowledge as it relates to action, or knowledge-in-action, is implicit. It does not involve conscious processes, so that actions, recognitions and judgements are skilled activities carried out spontaneously. Equally implicit is the knowledge the practitioner holds about the background, the history and the social embeddedness of the respective practice. This might lead one to conclude that professional action is basically a problem-solving activity where reflection and existing tacit knowledge are applied to emerging problems.

Schon however argued that this widespread understanding of professional practice is too limited and has to be extended to problem setting, a second order, more complex form of reflection, where the practitioner also considers wider concerns and implications of the problem, including for instance, institutional, political and social structures, which are external to the workplace itself (in our particular case, the classroom) but impact on it. At this stage, the practitioner sets in motion a process of re-naming and re-framing of the problem. Indeed, he or she might not even consider the issue at hand to be a problem anymore; though it is more likely that this meta-process will provide the learner with a different type of problem requiring a different type of solution.

Reflexivity and conscious analysis become even more necessary when the professional is confronted with new situations and as a consequence has to change or acquire new practices. Though the individual perceives the new situation to be unique in the first instance, to make sense of it requires its assimilation into existing frameworks of rules and resources. People do this by looking for similarities and differences. Schon understood the process of learning as cyclical with successive iterations of comparing new and familiar experiences with well-established routines of thinking, many of which the learner (in our case the teacher–practitioner) may have difficulty with bringing to consciousness. In professional practice, however, the individual also interacts with and acts upon the environment and attempts to make sense of it in an experimental fashion that involves the following non-sequential processes: exploring the possibilities inherent in the problem; developing a series of action steps; testing them out to see if they fit the problem; and evaluating the more successful solutions to develop working hypotheses. Experimenting in practice then is both reflective and transactional. The teacher is at the same time testing out new hypotheses and seeking to change the external setting in which the problem is embedded.

Professional development in this model is therefore a process of reflection in action with different degrees of complexity and reflection on action where teachers have to be encouraged to experiment with and explore new practices, contents and procedures in their actual workplace contexts, and to think about their relevance, usefulness and viability. Reflection, however, can be greatly increased through collaborative meaning making, dialogue and discussion between different practitioners who can add alternative perspectives, ideas and experiences. The exchanges between teachers from the same or different schools provide a further level of reflexivity to the teacher development programme, namely reflection on reflection in and on action.

An approach to professional development that emphasises reflection in action, on action, experimentation and collaboration stands in stark contrast to common formal modes of professional development where teachers are asked to reflect on their progress against a set of descriptors provided for them from an external source, and then have to plan and execute action steps with the intention of improving their performance. This fits better the executive technician model that we identified earlier. This is a limited form of meta-reflection that suffers from the disadvantage that the teacher may feel that they do not own the process and that the set of descriptors are not written at the required level of particularity to enable them to improve their performance. The ideal model of professional development presented here therefore encourages teachers to find appropriate and justified ways to implement the acquired knowledge in their own practice setting. To this end, it brings together three types of knowledge (Jackson and Temperley, 2006: 5), namely the accumulated experience-based and context-specific knowledge practitioners hold, external 'practical and theoretical public knowledge which might serve to frame, support, structure, illuminate or (critically) challenge existing contours of knowledge and training', and 'new knowledge' created by individuals and groups of teachers, for example, through action research.

Although the concept of the 'reflective practitioner', as developed by Schon, has become extremely influential in teacher education and training, the concept has also lost some of its original meaning. It is therefore important to make concrete suggestions about how reflexivity can be fostered in professional development workshops. Teachers familiarise themselves with the new ideas, their objectives, rationale, contents and procedures, and experiment with these elements in their actual classrooms. They engage in processes of developing their professional practice and at the same time adapt, refine and contribute to the refinement of the curriculum that they are implementing. Teachers reflect on their past and current teaching practice, for example, through a teacher portfolio or a professional autobiography, two genres in which they can explore, either privately or publicly, their own development, positive and critical experiences which have shaped their career, changing goals, values and expectations among other issues. They reflect upon their professional practices, routine activities and values in their institutional, socio-cultural, economic and political context, i.e. from different angles and perspectives. This has the potential to encourage the redefinition and re-conceptualisation of problems and their potential solutions.

Practitioners share teaching materials and exchange views and experiences of particular pedagogic strategies with peers. This allows them to get to know alternatives and to amplify their own pool of resources. They look beyond their own classroom through peer coaching, team teaching and classroom observation. Again, they are able to learn from others and contribute to the learning of their peers. Teachers are introduced to and employ methods of analysing classroom interaction and communication in relation to contextual affordances and constraints. They can seek feedback from their students who are an important source for their development, for example, through individual and group journals and discussions. Teachers engage in collaborative inquiry, for example, through action research. They share the generated knowledge so that it can inform practices in other schools and contribute to a pool of resources for all the teachers involved.

One area that attempts to overcome the gap between theory and teaching practice by involving teachers as agents in actual investigations is action research. Action research seeks to solve practical, mostly classroom-based problems and to foster the practical judgement of actors in real situations. Involving teachers in curriculum development and implementation allows practitioners to 'own' the knowledge they generate. It is assumed that innovation is more likely to be accepted if teachers are involved in the design of materials that is relevant for their students and adapted to their needs. Since curriculum development depends upon a high level of professional judgement, it is appropriate to build professional development round a teacher-as-local-expert model.

Professional learning is both a process internal to the individual (construction) and social (enculturation), as it requires participation in socially organised practices in particular communities (Borko, 2004). Effective professional development therefore not only encourages reflection and lifelong learning on an individual level but also collaboration through teacher learning communities. Such communities share and critically interrogate their practices in a collaborative, inclusive and growth promoting fashion and ultimately pursue the common goal of improving their effectiveness for the benefit of their students (Mitchell and Sackney, 1998). There are several additional reasons why such communities are appropriate. They are a non-threatening venue allowing teachers to notice weaknesses in their content and pedagogic knowledge and get help with these deficiencies. They are embedded in the day-to-day realities of teachers' classrooms and schools, and thus provide a time and place where teachers can hear real-life stories from colleagues that show the benefits of adopting these techniques in situations similar to their own. Without that kind of local reassurance, there is little chance teachers will risk upsetting the prevailing status quo. Even though it had limitations, the old arrangement at least allowed teachers to maintain some form of order and matched the expectations of most principals and colleagues. As teachers adjust their practice, they are risking both disorder and less-than-accomplished performance on the part of their students and themselves.

Being a member of a community of teacher-learners engaged together in a change process provides the support teachers need to take such risks. In short, teacher-learning communities provide a forum for supporting teachers in converting the curricular reform into lived practices within their classrooms. Collaborative enquiry and learning has transformative potential as it involves larger sections of the teaching force and enhances their capacity to deal with change. School-embedded teacher learning communities are sustained over time, allowing change to occur developmentally. The knowledge that is created will also be disseminated in real time. The collaborative enquiry is an inclusive activity and thus contributes to the generation and maintenance of a learning organisation (Street and Timperley, 2005). The involvement of the entire institution in a curricular reform is particularly important in contexts where a mismatch exists between the operational logic of the administrative and the academic system, usually at the expense of the latter. Collaborative enquiry creates professional knowledge that is potentially relevant to larger populations of teachers and can hence be fruitfully transferred to other schools.

Teacher Training Curricula

This model of productive learning environments also has implications for teacher training curricula. A curriculum indicates what is intended should happen in a programme of learning and the circumstances in which these activities can take place. The activities referred to here are learning activities; a curriculum is a collection of exercises and tasks that culminates in learning of one type or another. There are two principles which structure the choice and order of content within such a curriculum: a spiral element or a re-visiting of concepts, skills or dispositions at a higher level of intensity and at a later point in the programme of study; and theory transfer from theory to practice and from sites of learning to sites of application. The first of these is the need to incorporate a spiral element into the curriculum:

> a metaphoric spiral in which at some simple level a set of ideas or operations were introduced in a rather intuitive way and, once mastered in that spirit, were then revisited and reconstructed in a more formal or operational way, then being connected with other knowledge, the mastery at this stage then being carried one step higher to a new level of formal or operational rigour and to a broader level of abstraction and comprehensiveness. (Bruner, 1996: 3–4)

And the second refers to the relationships between experience, theory or concept development (in the three different domains of knowledge, skill and disposition), developing strategies for the application of this theory or set of concepts (including the development of knowledge, skill and dispositional application capacities), applying these learning and practice skills, strategies and plans for action in real-life educational settings, and evaluating these practices with the purpose of changing them (including the development and use of knowledge, skill and dispositional deployment capacities). The effect is to move the student teacher into the centre of the practice and away from the periphery.

In this curriculum model, the learning intentions of the pre-service or in-service programmes do not specify how the knowledge, skills and dispositions should be taught. As a consequence the teacher-trainer needs to reconceptualise each learning intention into a programme of learning or action learning set. Pedagogic approaches and strategies range from didactic to imitative to reflective and meta-reflective action learning sets. A pedagogic approach needs to: specify the circumstances in which it can be used in the specific learning environment;

specify the resources and technologies needed to allow that learning to take place; specify the type of relationship between teacher and student, and student and student, to effect that learning; specify a theory of learning that explains how that construct (i.e. knowledge set, skill or disposition) can be assimilated; and develop a theory of transfer held by the teacher, that is, explain how the learning which has taken place in a particular set of circumstances (i.e. a classroom, with a set of learners, in a particular way, with a particular theory of learning underpinning it, and so forth) can transfer to other environments in other places and times.

In this model, learning outcomes are distinguished from assessment approaches. It is therefore important that the outcome is not compromised in any way by whether it can or cannot be used as a testable construct. An assessment practice specifies those knowledge sets, skills or dispositions that a student is required to have, and which are expressed in such a way that they can be tested in a controlled environment, such as an examination. The principal problem with assessment protocols is that testing a person's knowledge, skills and aptitudes is likely to have washback effects on the original knowledge or skill set. Instead of the assessment acting merely as a descriptive device, it also acts in a variety of ways to transform the curriculum it is seeking to measure. Washback effects work on a range of objects and in different ways. So, for example, there are washback effects on the curriculum, on teaching and learning, on the capacity of the individual and more fundamentally on the structures of knowledge, though these four mechanisms are frequently conflated in the minds of educational stakeholders. Micro-washback effects work directly on the person, whereas macro-washback effects work directly on institutions and systems, which then subsequently have an impact on individuals within those institutions and systems. Finally, a student may have to reframe their knowledge or skill set to fit the test, and therefore the assessment of their mastery of this knowledge or skill is not a determination of their competence, but a determination of whether they have successfully understood how to rework their capacity to fit the demands of the examination technology. As a result teaching to the test occurs and the curriculum is narrowed to accommodate those learning outcomes that can more easily be assessed.

The reason for separating out learning intentions from assessment approaches is now clear. If these assessment approaches are the same as learning intentions, then this is likely to have a detrimental and reductionist effect on the curriculum and more importantly on the type and content of learning that takes place. However, there are different needs within a system of education, and one of those needs is that at certain points in time national, state and district educational bodies need to have information about how well the system is doing. This is a very different process from improving learning with an individual student teacher. However, there must be some connecting link between actual learning and reporting, so that the latter doesn't distort the former, and this is the role of learning aims and intentions.

This does not mean that assessment is not an essential part of any teaching and learning programme. Assessment for learning can be presented as five key strategies and one cohering idea. The five key strategies are: engineering effective classroom discussions, questions and learning tasks; clarifying and sharing learning intentions and criteria for success; providing feedback that moves learners forward; activating students as the owners of their own learning; and activating students as instructional resources for one another. The cohering idea is that evidence about student learning is used to adapt instruction to better meet learning needs; in other words, that teaching is adaptive to the student's learning needs (cf. Black and Wiliam, 2009). This ties closely together assessment and learning.

Learning and assessment practices on a teacher training programme can be regarded as formative if there is evidence of the student's achievement; that evidence is elicited, interpreted and used by the teacher-trainer, the individual student and their fellow students; and such evidence is used by the teacher-trainer with the specific intention of deciding on the subsequent steps in the teaching-and-learning process (i.e. 'instruction' with the intention of further developing learning). The interaction between the teacher-trainer and their student(s) is formative when it influences the learner's cognition: the teacher-trainer's external stimulus and feedback triggers an internal production by the individual student (cf. Black and Wiliam, 2009).

This model of a pre-service teacher training programme then makes a clear distinction between summative and formative assessment. Learning outcomes can be used in a number of different ways, with different consequences. They can be used to determine whether and in what way the individual is meeting them, as well as providing information about how the individual can perform better in the future. (This requires a learning intention having attached to it a pedagogic approach or strategy.) Or they can be used to summarise levels of achievement at group, institution or national levels. (This requires a learning intention to be translated into an assessment protocol.) In summary, they can be used summatively or formatively. If these two functions are combined, then the curriculum is liable to be attenuated.

In order to raise standards of achievement (i.e. increased levels of knowledge, enhanced skill levels and dispositional improvements), the following need to be taken into consideration: a minimisation of washback effects; an emphasis on curriculum, rather than assessment, driven reform; the preservation of the curriculum as the principal driver of a teacher training programme rather than what can be most easily assessed; a clear separation of the evaluative and learning functions in any educational reform; a clear set of curriculum specifications, expressed as learning intentions or curriculum standards; and the use of assessment devices for determining individual and group levels of achievement which are different from those assessment devices connected specifically to the learning process.

Teaching and Learning Models

A general model of teaching and learning can be characterised as a scaffolding process. Scaffolding essentially means an aid that is developed and offered to the learner by a more experienced person in support of the learning process with a focus on learning objectives. It has a number of characteristics: it is a temporary support; it is offered to the learner in relation to specific tasks that they are asked to perform, those tasks being derived from the learning outcomes; the learner is unlikely to complete the task without it; and the scaffold is provided to the student teacher by the teacher-trainer in their capacity as 'expert' in relation to the satisfactory completion of the task.

Scaffolding involves the following processes (Tharp and Gallimore, 1991): modelling, i.e. offering behaviour for imitation; feedback, i.e. providing information on a performance as it compares to a standard; instructing, i.e. requesting specific actions; questioning, i.e. requesting a verbal response that helps by producing a mental operation that the learner cannot or would not produce alone; cognitive structuring, i.e. providing explanations; and task structuring, i.e. chunking, segregating, sequencing, or otherwise structuring a task into or from components. While almost any learning aid can be a scaffold, scaffolding in teaching takes place only when the teacher-trainer provides specific help that meets the following criteria: contingency, i.e. the teacher-trainer's support is attuned to the student teacher's current state of understanding; the student teacher accomplishes the task with the teacher-trainer's situated help, and the student teacher performs the task independently; fading, i.e. the level and amount of support is gradually withdrawn from the student-teacher; and transfer of responsibility, i.e. the student-teacher takes increasing control of their own learning in the performance of a task.

The efficacy of scaffolding is influenced by the teacher-trainer's thoughtful combination of techniques and tasks, and the extent to which the teacher-trainer provides their students with multiple chances to engage with the relevant concepts and 'high-order' thinking processes. Teacher-trainers need to appreciate the different levels of scaffolding (i.e. intense, moderate and minimum) and become skilled in applying them accordingly, providing more support when a particular student struggles with a specific task and reducing help as they collect evidence that the student is now proficient in that task (Leat and Nichols, 1997). Technology-based scaffolds are regarded as valuable to support procedural tasks and to offer suitable cues for meta-cognitive processing. They also help by freeing up some of the teacher-trainer's attention in the training institute classroom, allowing them to give more attention to their students' reasoning. This allows a greater degree of personalisation in the learning process.

It is possible to identify a range of teaching and learning mechanisms or action sets. The first of these is observation, and this is where the teacher performs the action which the learner is required to imitate in the classroom, and then later in the context of application. Three types are noted: a live model involving a demonstration or acting out of the behaviours to be learnt; a verbal instructional model where this comprises descriptions and explanations of behaviours; and a symbolic model, i.e. scenario learning, plays, etc. These are stimuli for learning. The skills required of the student are: observing a performance by the teacher, whether live modelling, verbal instruction or symbolic modelling; comparing the performance with an embodied form of that display already held by the learner; adjusting their current construct through modification or substitution; practice by the student whilst being supported within the artificial environment; practice by the student without support within the artificial environment; transferring the skill to the real environment whilst being supported; and consolidation without support through use in the real environment (cf. Bandura, 1977).

With coaching the focus is on a series of steps: modelling by the expert; coaching whilst the learner practises; scaffolding where the learner is supported during the initial stages with that support gradually being withdrawn as the learner becomes more proficient (coaching here involves the teacher in identifying for the learner deviations from the model in the performance of the learner, and then supporting the learner as they make attempts to correct this performance); articulation by the learner of that process; reflection on those processes and comparison with the expert's reasons for action; and exploration where the learner undertakes the various activities without support.

Goal clarity is a component of productive learning environments. To that end, teachers need to provide learners with explicit statements and explanations about the instructional objectives in a lesson or series of lessons. Goal clarity has three learner-focused aspects: explanations about how they are expected to perform the tasks assigned to them; opportunities for them to grasp what is expected of them; and reflections about their capacity as self-directed learners in the completion of the task.

Goal-oriented teaching requires that the teacher undertakes specific actions to ensure goal clarity and a focus on task completion at three stages of the learning process: at the beginning, setting learning goals and providing learners with a model of the meta-cognitive strategies to start the task; in the middle or during the lesson, monitoring and assessing their goal progress, motivating learners to look for explanations by means of exploration and supporting them when they struggle, for example, by suggesting relevant learning strategies and giving them personalised feedback such as how to adjust those strategies; and at the conclusion, providing learners with an overall assessment of their goal progress, motivating them to extend their efforts, to persist and to keep adjusting their strategies, and developing new goals as they fulfil the old ones.

Mentoring supports the informal transmission of knowledge, social capital or psychosocial resources. It is usually conducted face-to-face and involves a relationship between two people, one of which is considered to have greater knowledge, wisdom or experience. Five possible mentoring techniques have been identified: supporting the student and even taking part in the same activity and learning side-by-side with the learner; preparing the student for the future even if they are not ready or able to learn what is being offered to them in the present; catalysing learning, provoking a different way of thinking, a change in identity or a re-ordering of values; showing through personal example; and finally, helping and supporting the learner in reflecting back on their previous learning (cf. Aubrey and Cohen, 1995).

Peer learning is defined as learning from and with the learner's peers. The other forms of learning comprise unequal relations between the teacher and the learner. Here the assumption is made that the learning relationship is between equals, and thus a different form of learning is implied. Examples of this type of learning include: affective support – being offered emotional support if learning proves to be difficult and this is always a better form of support if given by someone who is going through the same learning process; dyadic performance confrontations – learning is provoked by confrontational exchanges between students so that each student can test their theories, ideas and constructs against those held by learners engaging in the same form of learning; pair-problem-solving – here learning is enabled through cooperation between two learners of roughly equal standing, so that in a problem-solving exercise, better solutions are forthcoming because there are two problem-solvers rather than one; reciprocal peer tutoring – non-expert tutoring between equals has the advantage of each person being able to make their own evaluation of the advice being offered unencumbered by status or hierarchy; and scripted cooperative dyads – here peer engagement is focused on the joint production of a script, artefact, performance or text with the result that alternative and new interpretations/readings are forthcoming.

A simulation is a reproduction of an event or activity, conducted outside the environment in which that event or activity usually takes place. Simulations can be produced through computer games, role-plays, scenarios, presentations and affective and conceptual modelling. The purpose of this learning process is to simulate a real event, and this is to allow the person or persons taking part in that simulation to explore it, to experiment within it, to understand the process, to begin the process of internalisation, to experience, albeit in a limited way, the emotions and feelings that would normally accompany the experience in real life, and fundamentally, to allow learning to take place through trial and error and making mistakes in safe situations, which do not have the consequences they would have in real-life situations. Simulations compress time and remove extraneous detail. They are immersive learning experiences, where skills and performances can be enhanced in a way that is not possible outside the simulation.

Instructional learning, Gagné (1985) suggests, has nine steps. The teacher needs to gain the attention of the group of learners. This can be done by asking questions or addressing the purposes of the learning programme. The teacher then informs the learners of the objectives of the learning exercise, i.e. what it is intended should be learnt. The teacher needs to stimulate recall of prior learning amongst the group of learners, so that the new information is related productively to previous and current learning. Content is now presented to the students, and this has to be carefully structured or scaffolded, so that it can be accessed by them. The next event is a performance relating to the institutional objectives and this needs to be elicited from the student in an appropriate format. Feedback needs to be provided which is a comment on the student's performance and allows corrective action to take place. The new performance is then assessed in order to determine if the desired performance has taken place. Students apply that knowledge in appropriate ways.

Conceptual learning focuses on the re-forming of conceptual schema that the learner has about the world and in the particular case here, about those conceptual matters relating to schools, classrooms and teaching-learning processes. Learning is complex and potentially rich and rewarding, where the student is presented with a mass of information, ideas, schema, opinions from a number of different sources (i.e. books, articles, lectures, seminars, emails, eseminars, personal communications and so on). What the learner does is shape this mass of information, and this shaping can take a number of different forms: partial shaping, complete shaping, discarding with no replacement, confusion, on-going, going backwards and forwards and so on. Shaping takes place against a scholarly background, aspects of which may or may not be implicit and where some but not all of its aspects can be surfaced for deliberation. For individuals mediating between their various multiple identities, conceptual learning is irredeemably social, embedded and selective. So the learner has to absorb some of the ideas they are presented with and discard or partially discard others. Even if the student is prepared to operate through a notion of multiple identities, they are still selecting, filtering, endorsing, rejecting, enhancing and discarding.

The Learning Cycle, developed by David Kolb (1984), is based on the belief that deep learning (learning for real comprehension) comes from a sequence of experience, reflection, abstraction and active testing. Reflection is a form of evaluative thinking. It is applied to ideas for which there is no obvious solution and is largely based on the further processing of knowledge and understanding and possibly emotions that we already possess. It is thus a second-order internal activity, which can in certain circumstances be transformed into a learning strategy. There are some optimum conditions for reflection: time and space, a good facilitator, a supportive curricular or institutional environment, and an emotionally supportive environment. A number of tasks encourage reflection: ill-structured, 'messy' or real-life situations; asking the 'right' kinds of questions because there are no clear-cut answers; setting challenges to promote reflection; setting tasks that challenge learners to integrate new learning into previous learning; setting tasks that demand the ordering of thoughts; and setting tasks that require evaluation.

Meta-cognitive learning refers to learners' awareness of their own knowledge and their ability to understand, control and manipulate their own cognitive processes. However, most meta-cognitive processes can be placed within three categories (cf. Harris and Graham, 1999). The first is meta-memorisation. This refers to the learners' awareness of their own memory systems and their ability to deploy strategies for using their memories effectively. The second is meta-comprehension. This refers to the learners' ability to monitor the degree to which they understand information being communicated to them, to recognise failures to comprehend, and to employ repair strategies. And the third is self-regulation. This term refers to the learner's ability to make adjustments in their own learning processes. The concept of self-regulation overlaps with meta-memorisation and meta-comprehension; its focus is on the capacity of the learners themselves to monitor their own learning (without external stimuli or persuasion) and to act independently.

Using a problem-solving pedagogy, the learner finds out for themselves rather than being given answers to problems. The learner is required to engage in a series of interrogative processes with regards to texts, people and objects in the environment, and come up with solutions to problems. The learner is also required to use the skills of: information retrieval, information synthesis and analysis, and knowledge organisation. The learner may come up with inadequate, incorrect and faulty syntheses and analyses. However, this is acceptable because the learning resides in the process rather than in the end product. Problem-solving learning involves the learner in judging their own work against a curriculum standard and engaging in meta-processes of learning (i.e. an understanding about processes of one's own learning; the development of learning pathways; the utilisation of formative assessment processes; the development of personal learning strategies; and the internalisation of the curriculum).

Practice is the act of rehearsing a behaviour over and over again, or engaging in an activity again and again. This reinforces, enhances and deepens the learning associated with the behaviour or activity. These learning practices and their deployment are logically derived from the learning object, i.e. the intentions of the learning programme or learning outcomes. Choosing between these teaching and learning processes depends on the nature of the object that it is intended should be learnt, for example, classroom communication skills.

India

These conceptions of teacher learning environments and teacher training curricula at pre-service and in-service levels can act as templates for examining real syllabi in the Indian context. A curriculum, as we suggested above, indicates what is intended should happen in a programme of learning and the circumstances in which these activities can take place. The activities referred to in these three Indian examples are learning activities; a curriculum is a collection of exercises and tasks that culminates in learning of one type or another.

The first of these three teacher training curricula is the Bachelor of Elementary Education Programme. This is a four-year integrated degree programme offered after the senior secondary stage of schooling in the University of Delhi. It attempts to integrate the study of subject knowledge, human development, pedagogical knowledge and communication skills. Currently the programme is being offered in eight women's colleges. The programme offers both compulsory and optional theory, compulsory practicum courses and a comprehensive school internship experience. The student is expected to study 19 theory courses during the four-year programme of study. Foundation courses on the programme offer an in-depth study of the processes of child development and learning; how the education of children is influenced by the social, political, economic and cultural contexts in which they grow and develop; techniques and processes of school organisation and management; educational theory; and issues and concepts specific to elementary education. In addition to developing theoretical constructs and frameworks of analysis, these courses also aim to cultivate skills to build relationships and to communicate as teachers.

Core courses offer the student an opportunity to reconstruct concepts learnt in school and to integrate them into a multi-disciplinary perspective. These also form the foundation for courses directly related to pedagogic expertise. Pedagogy courses provide a study of pedagogical theory and are designed to develop skills specific to the teaching of young children. Liberal study courses, which form an important part of the overall package of courses, are designed to enrich the knowledge base, to allow for further study in the discipline and in the pedagogies in which students opt to specialise. The optional courses offered in the fourth year aim to provide specialised support to the student teacher. In addition, there is a range of practicum courses.

Practicum courses are crafted so as to allow a variety of experiences with children within and outside the elementary school. In addition, students are expected to acquire a wide range of professional skills including drama, craft, developing curricular material, classroom management, systematic observations, documentation and evaluation. Performing and Fine Arts, Crafts and Physical Education are integrated into the curriculum in the same spirit as they are in the elementary school curriculum. They enable the student to experience and understand the learning process in a holistic manner, rather than confining it to the 'cognitive' domain.

The School Contact Programme establishes the first contact of the student teachers with children. This first experience allows the student teacher to engage with issues of planning and organising creative activities for children within the school. They also explore ways of organising meaningful interaction with children outside the school. The student teachers are given the opportunity to develop their capabilities in relation to communicating and developing a positive attitude towards children and teaching. The activity of observing children is designed to help establish a crucial link between theoretical concepts and on-the-ground realities. Through the systematic observation and study of children in different settings, the student teacher is expected to develop ways of understanding children and how they learn. Through a process of self-reflection and analysis in self-development workshops, students sharpen their abilities and learn to question, and to be critical and reflective, or at least this is the intention.

Placement in schools forms a major component of the fourth year of the Bachelor of Elementary Education Programme. Student teachers actively engage in teaching elementary school children. Functioning as regular teachers, the student teachers are encouraged to attempt to translate their knowledge base and professional skills into classroom practice and then reflect on what actually happened. The student teachers are required to complete projects based on themes arising out of their school experience. This enables them to acquire basic research skills of systematic observation, documentation and analysis. Tutorials, which are an integral part of the programme, help the student teachers to build connections between theory, observations and classroom teaching. The student teachers are expected to present term papers and participate in discussions. Colloquia are structured to include activities on children's literature, story-telling, drama and music; organising teaching and learning resource centres and seminar presentations of school experiences. Colloquia are an essential part of all the four years of study. Finally, seminars and workshops are an integral part of the programme of study.

The programme has many strengths. It separates out and clearly distinguishes subject knowledge, pedagogical knowledge and practice-based knowledge and skills. It suggests a dynamic and productive form of pedagogy with an emphasis on reflection and practice. For example, the programme is:

> ... designed to compel the teacher-educator to shift her role from one of giving answers and providing a technical-rationalist view of knowledge to elevating ambiguity and helping students develop from a position of dependence to autonomy.

It treats seriously the need to connect theory and practice and thus translate theory into practice, by providing a possible mechanism for doing this. It offers a structured and progressive route into the practicum. Its contents (usually expressed as knowledge, skills and dispositions) cover most of the required areas for teacher training.

However, there are some weaknesses in the design of the curriculum and their identification in relation to the models of professional learning and teacher training curricula that we have described above. In the syllabus there are some omissions of important content elements. For example, there are few references to dispositional learning, nor is there any real discussion of professional (including ethical) standards, and how to use these at the site of practice. We have already suggested that teacher training programme syllabuses should distinguish between: learning aims and intentions; content knowledge; teaching and learning approaches; and logistics of use, i.e. when and where they should be used, and make appropriate connections between them. This is an area of concern in this syllabus. Another concern is a tendency to conflate knowledge, skills and dispositions, and to omit references to teaching and learning approaches that are appropriate for these three different elements. This is an important curriculum principle, and neglect of it results in didactic and unproductive pedagogic practices here and round the world.

The syllabus does not specify how formative and summative forms of assessment work in different ways, and how each is important in any pre-service curriculum. In conflating the two, or ignoring the issue, learning is subsequently impoverished. Any curriculum (either at pre-service or in-service levels) needs to focus on learning, and in this case learning how to be a teacher (pre-service). There is a tendency in this syllabus to give prominence to forms of assessment (i.e. examinations) which are not suitable for assessing many of the knowledge constructs, skills and dispositions associated with pre-service teacher training. The syllabus does not pay enough attention to learning processes and certainly there is a lack of fit between learning intentions or curriculum standards and learning approaches. What this means is that inappropriate teaching and learning approaches may be used, with the consequence that training programmes become poor vehicles for delivering these very important learning aims and intentions.

We also looked at a series of model curricula developed by the Indian National Council for Teacher Education. These included: the revised BEd Curriculum and the revised DECCE Curriculum. The BEd (secondary) programme is designed for an annual pattern of implementation. However, it can be delivered in a semester pattern consisting of two semesters of about 18 weeks each including admission, preparatory holidays and examination, assuming six working days in a week. Reorganisation into a semester pattern has to take account of the scheduling of the internship in teaching and courses that are preparatory to internship. It consists of five areas of study: Foundations of Education, Pedagogical Knowledge, Pedagogical Content Knowledge, School Based Experiences and Add-on Courses such as Language Proficiency Workshop, and ICT–Skill Development.

The model programme has the following general objectives:

1. The student teacher understands the central concepts, tools of inquiry, and structures of the disciplines and can create learning experiences that make these aspects of subject matter meaningful;
2. The student teacher understands how children learn and develop, how they differ in their approaches to learning, and creates learning opportunities that are adapted to diverse learners and learning contexts;

3. The student teacher plans learning experiences that are based on the learner's existing proficiency, interests, experiences including misconceptions and errors; and an understanding of how students come to view, develop and make sense of subject matter contained in the learning experiences;

4. The student teacher uses knowledge of effective verbal, non-verbal and media communication techniques to foster active inquiry, collaboration and supportive interaction in the classroom;

5. The student teacher understands and uses formal and informal assessment strategies to evaluate and ensure the continuous intellectual, social and physical development of the learner;

6. The student teacher develops their self-identity as a teacher through school based experiences and reflective practices that continually evaluate the effects of his/her choices and actions. (National Council of Educational Research and Training, 2014a)

In an attempt to move away from didactic and theory-laden forms of delivery, student-teachers are required on the programme to engage with the material in a variety of ways: through lectures and discussions, where the teacher-educator provides a platform for a review of experiences, and an opportunity to develop insights into the disciplinary knowledge base and relate them to the realities of school life; through focused readings and reflections, where student teachers are led through focused readings on various themes with questions inviting reflections either individually or in small groups; and through observation-documentation-analysis, which comprises simulated and real school/community experiences arranged for the student-teachers to observe. In addition, they are required to engage with the programme: through creating documents in the form of a record/journal/diary and analysing them with the intention of revisiting their own understandings or developing new insights; through seminars where they undertake thematic/topical study, prepare analyses and make seminar presentations, followed by open-house discussions with a view to enhancing their knowledge base and repertory of skills in the area of presentation; through the development of case studies involving an in-depth and comprehensive study of a single or few cases; through in-school-based practicals, which comprise observations of an experienced practitioner, planning-implementing-receiving feedback from peers and their supervisor and reflection on their own performance; and through taking part in workshops, involving a series of learning experiences in a given performance area, engaging them in a modelling-practice-feedback sequence with a view to developing specified teaching competencies.

We have already identified some possible weaknesses in syllabuses such as these, for example, weak connections being made between curricular objectives and learning approaches. (This doesn't mean that teachers do not implicitly make appropriate connections in their actual practice; what it means is that such connections are neither properly articulated nor theorised in the teacher training curriculum.) A further point in relation to learning is that the learning approaches specified above lack detail in relation to what they are and how they can be applied, with the consequence that they either become detached from actual practice (e.g. teacher educators describe their practice as progressive but in fact operate with didactic and unproductive pedagogies) or they are both misdescribed and misapplied.

In the revised DECCE Curriculum, the proposed learning intentions or standards of the two-year Diploma in Early Childhood and Early Primary Teacher Education are that the student-teacher at the end of the programme will be able to:

1. Discuss the rights and developmental needs of children from conception to the age of eight years; analyse and reflect on the perspectives, priorities and challenges of early childhood and early primary education and the inter-relationship between the two;

2. Demonstrate insight into the interdependent processes of child development and learning and the implications for planning the curriculum; plan and implement such tasks to meet children's needs for health, protection, nutrition, education and development in age appropriate and contextually relevant ways;

3. Demonstrate skill sets appropriate for planning and transacting a play and activity-based learning curriculum from pre-school to early primary grades;

4. Network with parents, community and other organisations to generate awareness and seek this involvement in ECCE programmes;

5. Provide appropriate interventions to meet the requirements of an inclusive classroom;

6. Adapt the programme in accordance with the language and cultural diversity that comprise the Indian social fabric and many co-existing social realities and its challenges in the classroom;

7. Use local talents and skills and resources along with the contemporary use of computers in the classroom. (National Council of Educational Research and Training, 2014b)

There is an aspect of this proposed curriculum that successfully illustrates an important element of learning how to be a teacher, and this is the sequence of learning elements in relation to the practicum. The first element is where the learner (in this case, the student-teacher) observes a teacher in action and this is a live model involving a demonstration or acting out of the behaviours to be learnt. Away from the real-life setting the student-teacher then takes part in a simulation of the activity. This is followed by a planning process, which is intended to allow the student-teacher to develop the capacity to transfer those skills and dispositions to real-life settings, in this case the classroom, and this involves reflective and self-evaluative forms of learning. The student-teacher then practises those skills and dispositions in real-life settings but in a limited way and is supported in doing this. Finally, the student-teacher undertakes a full internship which incorporates all the elements of the actual practice.

Policy Implementation

Professional learning activities and new teacher training curricula practices in India need an implementation strategy. There are four dimensions to policy implementation: making sure that the reform programme is comprehensive, satisfactory and serviceable; understanding how the implementation site is currently constructed; specifying how the current implementation site will need to be changed to accommodate the new initiative; and determining how this new initiative can be institutionalised so that it functions effectively. We might want to call these four dimensions: the new programme structure; implementation sites; implementation capacity; and institutionalisation and sustainability processes.

The first element refers to the internal relations of the new practice that is to be transferred to a new setting (i.e. the new programme structure). As we suggested in Chapter 1, a model of a new productive practice (or reform) has a number of characteristics. It has a set of elements arranged in a logically coherent way (i.e. an arrangement of resources, functions and roles for people in the system, and accountability relationships). It has a causal narrative. And there is a rationale (substantive, ethical, practical and consequential) for the productive practice and for its implementation.

The second element of our change model is understanding how the system into which the new productive practice is to be implemented works. This means that the investigator/implementer needs to identify and evaluate how the system currently works; current arrangements of people and resources; current allocations of people to functions and roles; and current outputs from the system.

The third element refers to the new site of practice or the implementation site. In the first instance an account needs to be provided, which specifies the arrangements of resources in the new productive practice; possible changes to the arrangement of resources and people as a result of implementing the productive practice; the desired rate of change; and the intended effects of implementing the productive practice, i.e. planned consequences and possible unintended effects. These are speculations about what might happen and they refer to unplanned effects and strategies for minimising unintended outcomes if they occur.

The fourth and final stage is the institutionalising and sustainability process. It is important, in the first instance, to evaluate formatively the implementation of the productive practice to allow continuous monitoring of the initiative. Evaluative practices can be regarded as formative if evidence is gathered relating to the programme of activity being evaluated; that evidence is elicited, interpreted and used by the practitioner, the policy-maker or an interested party; and such evidence is used by them with the specific intention of deciding on the subsequent steps in the development of the productive practice. The productive practice is in a constant state of change and development.

The longevity and sustainability of the new productive practice in situ, and as it is being implemented, depends on resource arrangements, allocations of particular people to positions of responsibility, particular roles and arrangements of power and authority, the capacity of key people in the system, policy discourses and new policies.

This raises a number of questions about moral responsibility in making judgements about the person or people involved in the system that is being subject to the reform. Does the person (or persons) qualify as a moral agent (or moral agents)? Do they possess the general capacity to perform as a moral agent, where this refers to an ability to evaluate their reasons for doing this rather than that? Are the conditions in place in the educational system that allow the agent to perform in a way that conforms to their sense of moral accountability, i.e. have they performed it freely and were they allowed to exercise their moral culpability? And finally, have they taken sufficient account of the conditional nature of any decision-making they might want to engage in? This conditionality has four forms: social actors are relatively unaware of some of the conditions for their actions, that is, every action has a set of conditions underpinning it, for example, a speech act requires a language, vocabulary and grammar; they are unlikely to be able to predict all the consequences of their actions, so there are going to be unintended consequences; social actors may not be aware of much of their own knowledge and expertise, in other words, much of their knowledge is tacit, and thus they cannot, except with the greatest of difficulty, surface it in their accounts of their lives; and equally they may be motivated by unconscious forces and impulsions which they find great difficulty in articulating. A distinction can be drawn between attributability and responsibility as accountability (Aristotle, 1925), and this distinction rests on the difference between ascribing moral responsibility to a person or organisation because they or the organisation is formally responsible for their or its activities and only making someone or some organisation responsible if they were in a position to do something about it and thus effectively make a difference. This last involves a judgement about what is reasonable in attributing praise or blame to a person or organisation in the actual circumstances in which those activities were performed and about which that judgement is being made.

The next chapter examines issues that relate to leadership and devolved governance in education systems such as India.

5

SCHOOL AUTONOMY AND SCHOOL LEADERSHIP

This chapter addresses two closely connected sets of issues: the first is school autonomy and decentralisation, and the second is school leadership and capacity development. The two are connected because the structural change to autonomy and decentralisation both requires and stimulates reconsideration of how schools are led. Any discussion of 'leadership' invites consideration of questions regarding leading what, leading where and leading how; more explicitly, the aspects of the work of a school its leaders prioritise for their attention, the destination they are aiming to travel towards, and the methods and capabilities they will employ to do this. These constitute the elements and relations that are the essence of the particular productive practice that concerns the policy-maker when they are engaged in an act of policy-development or policy-borrowing and even more so when they are engaged in an act of policy-learning. The progressive implementation of decentralisation and school autonomy in numerous countries has been accompanied by continuously evolving thinking and practice in relation to these questions and issues.

These issues are more nebulous and complex than our other two focuses of policy learning. The preparation and career-long development of teachers relates to the quality of the most important direct input to formal schooling, and inclusive practices concern access to and the quality of learning experiences from the point of view of the learners. The issues which are the focuses for this chapter are of a second-order nature, being concerned with creating contextual organisational conditions and trajectories of change that their proponents believe assist improvements both to teaching and learning; although it is important to note that there have been other economic and political motivations for decentralising decision-making. Our interest in policy learning requires us to take a further step in analytical abstraction. This involves identifying what approaches to the implementation of school autonomy and school leadership development are most conducive to engendering beneficial learning.

School Autonomy, School Leadership and Policy Learning

The policy ideas summarised by the term 'school autonomy' emerged from the combination of four main developments, over a particular period of time, first reaching prominence in the 1980s, mainly in Anglo-Saxon countries. The four developments were: political interest in market forces as a driver of financial efficiency in public services; political prioritisation of developing human capital as a driver of global competitiveness; developments in communication technologies which made possible forms of school system organisation other than the model of classical bureaucracy; and the knowledge outputs of the school effectiveness movement within educational research. For the purposes of analysis, it is helpful to note that the first three of these developments were responses to changes in environmental conditions, including the economic factors of the rising cost of public services and the strength of global competition; the technological factor of information and communication technology (ICT) use within public administration; and in some regions, the demographic factor of rapidly growing school populations. In contrast, the school effectiveness movement generated changes in normative values, especially beliefs and expectations regarding educational outcomes. The institutional patterns of how schools are organised sit between patterns of change in environmental factors, and patterns of change in normative values. It was Holmes' (1981) contention, developed by Wilkins (2010, 2014) that challenges for policy-makers and administrators arise where changes in the institutional pattern are not synchronised with the pace of change in related factors in the environment (demographic, economic and technological) and the normative pattern (in relation to beliefs, values and expectations). This way of thinking is particularly useful when considering issues of policy learning across cultures. For example, approaches to school autonomy and school leadership developed in India, undertaken in the knowledge of practices developed mainly in economically advanced Anglo-Saxon countries, must take account of relevant differences both in environmental contexts and in values and expectations.

Normative values are certainly a factor affecting the choice of approach to decentralising decision-making in school systems. Lauglo (1996), contributing to a collection of studies comparing educational restructuring in Australia, Sweden, England and the USA, offered a framework for considering the implications of different forms of decentralisation. Lauglo proposed that the alternative to bureaucratic centralism might be found among four political rationales and four quality and efficiency rationales. In the first group were liberalism, federalism, popular localism and participatory democracy; in the second were pedagogic professionalism, management by objectives, market mechanisms and deconcentration. Each of these eight options carried different implications for the distribution of decision-making and for methods of monitoring and evaluation.

The policy ideas summarised by the term 'school leadership' evolved in the wake of thinking about school autonomy, broadly in the same places and over a similar period of time. For the purposes of policy learning across cultures it is important to recognise how patchy and recent this concept is. For most of the 300 years or so for which schools have been in operation, the notion of 'leadership' has not featured strongly. Schools and school systems have been *governed* and *administered*, and those words continue to describe the dominant mind-set in many school systems today. Over the history of schooling, there have of course been many pioneering educational thinkers. These have tended to be commented upon as reforming practitioners, making ground-breaking advances within the profession of pedagogy, comparable to the contributions of inventors, scientific discoverers, and notable philosophers, economists and thinkers in other fields. There has also, in the UK especially, been a strong tradition of religious involvement in the provision of schooling, including schools being run by the clergy, promoting an ethos including religious discipline which some might call spiritual and pastoral leadership. Notwithstanding those traditions, neither the 'thought leadership' in the professional practice of pedagogy, nor the pastoral leadership of the school as a community, were noticeably connected to what emerged as the mainstream notions of leadership which had their origins in military and industrial thinking.

This changed when research, especially within the school effectiveness movement, began to demonstrate that schools could make a difference to learning outcomes to a greater extent than had previously been assumed. This stimulated interest in the actions and practices of head teachers and other senior staff in schools, which achieved educational outcomes above the average in relation to student intake characteristics. The growth of school leadership literature drew heavily on the theories and literature of general management, for example, in fields such as strategic direction, human resource management and external relations, incorporating theories regarding leadership styles and the management of change.

To these were added the distinctly educational interest in theorising the leadership of learning. While the school leadership literature drew heavily on research within the school effectiveness paradigm, it drew equally heavily on research within the school improvement paradigm. The term 'school effectiveness' is often associated with the search for 'proven' replicable practices, with a focus on detailed practice inside classrooms which implement externally derived methods, preferably based on large-scale experimental studies, and hence favouring the top-down dissemination of knowledge. The term 'school improvement' is often associated with broader processes of beneficial change, which, while incorporating external support, are essentially institution-led, with teachers and school leaders playing a significant part in devising their own solutions, and contributing to the bottom-up growth of new knowledge.

In due course, constructive amalgamations of these viewpoints have been attempted, for example, White and Barber (1997), but the philosophical contradictions between these two standpoints remain, often leading to contradictory policies being pursued at the same time. Notwithstanding this, a broad consensus now exists among the Anglo-Saxon countries, and more widely, about the nature and purpose of school leadership. A number of countries have developed statements of standards of school leadership, which are consistent with each other, and derivative of key academic writings, including Leithwood et al. (1999). The key ideas include setting a vision, direction and high expectations; developing people; providing intellectual stimulation and modelling; leading for individual and organisational learning; and developing the organisation's structure, culture and community relationships.

This prevalent viewpoint has been challenged by a critical literature that draws attention to the real and significant difficulties of reconciling much mainstream leadership thinking with contexts and processes, which are truly educative. Smyth's (1989) constructive contribution on this point is picked up in the next section.

Debate in both fields – school autonomy and school leadership – has been complicated by the way in which both concepts have suffered partial political appropriation. In the case of school autonomy, a bedrock of supportive consensus has been partially overlain with a veneer of political argument with regards to whether it does or does not, should or should not, also support agendas of promoting market competition and/or privatisation of the school system. In the case of school leadership, consensus regarding much of the research-based theory has been overlain by political pressure favouring an aggressively hard management style, supported by equally hard accountability and high-stakes testing.

It will be clear from the accounts of research and practice referred to in this chapter that a great deal of learning has been engendered by increased school autonomy, not least through the school leadership development activity that has accompanied autonomy. The learning has included much that was unplanned, and also some lessons about the implementation of large, complex reforms to school systems. For the purposes of our model of policy learning it is necessary to probe the dynamics of the learning processes involved, in order to understand the conditions that are most conducive to positive learning.

Getting inside our core concerns involves making sense of highly complex changes, which in turn requires the selection of analytical lenses. In addition to theories of change, this chapter explores the learning that has arisen from school autonomy from organisational, spatial and pedagogic viewpoints. To balance the temptations of post-hoc rationalisation, perspectives from different periods and different countries (i.e. potential productive locations for learning) over the last 30 years have been drawn upon.

Pedagogy and Policy Learning

To explore processes and contexts that are conducive to learning by different elements within a diverse group of policy-makers, officials, school leaders and expert professionals supporting school system leadership, it is necessary to take up positions in relation to pedagogy. In this chapter, the word 'pedagogy' applies to learners of all ages, because all teaching and learning strategies should take proper account of learners' characteristics, contexts and priorities. So we reject Knowles' (1970) application of the term 'andragogy' to learning among adults, but we do attach weight to the importance of prior experience to adult learners, along the lines of Kolb (1984). We agree with Johnson (1996) that education leadership is fundamentally an educative process. Martin (2011: 2–3) observes that education is the process of encounter between individual capacities and culture, *in which both are changed*. This recognition that the impact of learning is two-way – that the learner changes not only themselves but also those with whom they have interacted during the process of learning – is of fundamental significance to the model of policy learning.

Cultural contexts differ regarding the extent to which people at different levels of position-power are prepared to learn together and are prepared to be changed not only by their own learning but by the learning of others. Senior policy-makers in very hierarchical societies may prefer to do their own learning in private, at the hands of international consultants, and then to present their fledgling understanding authoritatively to those at lower levels. That approach severely limits the possibilities for system-wide constructive learning.

There remains a tension between anything that might be called a pedagogy of professional learning and the prevailing culture of managerialism. Smyth (1989), as noted earlier, wondered whether the notion of school staffs being divided into leader and led was anti-educational. Instead, he sought to explore how people working in a school setting 'might actively assist one another in uncovering meaning in what they do, while investing in them the capacity to change, improve and transform those practices' (Smyth, 1989: 179).

Developments and Commentaries

In one respect the development of school autonomy differs from some other topics within the field of education. It has often been observed that policy-makers, practitioners and researchers exist in different communities, speak different languages, and have different focuses of interest, and that these differences help to explain why research has had such little impact on policy and practice. While that is true up to a point, a distinctive feature of the development of school autonomy is how much boundary-crossing has happened to bridge these divides. Key policy entrepreneurs have also been key academic researchers, whilst also maintaining close practitioner involvement.

Thus any review of the field must mention Brian Caldwell, who had significant involvement as a policy adviser in the development of school autonomy in Alberta (Canada) and subsequently in Victoria (Australia), and who has been a pioneering thinker and activist on the subject over an extended period (see, for example, Caldwell and Hayward, 1998; Caldwell, 2000). Similarly Ben Levin has combined policy and academic roles. Among outputs spanning an extended period, Levin (2001) analysed a suite of reform programmes in five settings: England, New Zealand, Manitoba (Canada), Alberta (Canada) and Minnesota (USA). Levin's (2001) analyses of devolved school management in England and New Zealand are particularly relevant to this chapter. Levin's insights are interesting because as well as academic work his career included periods as deputy minister (chief civil servant) for education in Ontario, and previously, in Manitoba.

In the same way, it is helpful that over the relevant historical period (essentially the late 1980s to the present time) we have, between us, practical experience of leading education reform and innovation as well as experience as parliamentary lobbyists and advisers to politicians in the UK and other countries. There is also a generation of commentators whose working lives have spanned the whole development from its outset. Distinguished names within that group include Ron Glatter in relation to the UK and Judith Chapman in relation to Australia. Glatter (2012) reviewed 40 years of developing thinking in the UK on the twin subjects of school autonomy and school accountability, presenting insights that resonate entirely with our own experiences and previous writings. Chapman's commentaries on school autonomy in Australia offer a similarly longitudinal perspective (see, for example, Chapman et al., 1996; Chapman and Aspin, 1997).

The significance of the points in the last few paragraphs is that so much boundary-crossing and prolonged first-hand observation gives additional levels of authenticity to the story. It also makes it easier for commentators, including ourselves, to distinguish policy from politics. The latter refers to the daily gladiatorial contest of linguistic acrobatics and presentational tactics that politicians have to employ to maintain an impression that they are controlling the agenda and heading in a desirable direction. We have presented in Chapter 3 our understanding of 'policy', which is broadly consistent with that of Rizvi and Lingard (2010).

The set of productive practices that were central to the research and development project conducted by us and in conjunction with Save the Children India (Terano et al., 2011) included, in their search for international productive practices in education, improvements to leadership practices and decentralised forms of administration and governance within the school system. Within the scope of this chapter, Terano and colleagues noted the importance of training school principals not only as organisational administrators, but also as educational and community leaders.

This was a prerequisite for moving effectively to school autonomy in increasingly decentralised systems, which also required education civil servants to develop new capacities. Terano et al. (2011) selected, as jurisdictions within which productive practices in these fields were evident, England, for leadership development of school principals; Ontario for systemic reform; and Victoria (Australia) and New Zealand, in both cases for decentralisation of decision-making.

Tension between Decentralisation and Accountability

Policies are not implemented in isolation, and a recurrent theme of this chapter is how the decentralisation of school systems has usually been accompanied by apparently contradictory policies of centralised accountability. This makes it very difficult to evaluate the effects of school decentralisation on its own, because it is impossible to disaggregate the effects of concurrent policies. That governments find it necessary to pursue apparently contradictory policies is one of the givens of modern political life; a subject explored by Aspin (1996) in relation to the education policies of Australia and England.

Lundgren and Mattsson (1996) probed the relationship between decentralisation and school improvement from a Swedish perspective but taking account of developments in many other countries. Lundgren and Mattsson observed that 'improvement' (often, in fact, more accurately seen as adjustments to align with topical priorities) may be driven externally or internally. In the former case, the school as an institution must adjust to the demands of wider society. In the latter case, the school pushes forward with developments in practice that are ahead of the norms and expectations of society. Thus, as Kraftl (2013) has more recently observed, schools may be both derivative and constitutive of society.

Lundgren and Mattsson traced the economic developments of the 1950s and 1960s, including the adoption of human capital theory at a time of population growth, which led to heavy investment in the expansion and development of school systems. In this period, the rational paradigm favoured centrally administered reform, enabling plans to be both made and implemented – a preference which fitted well in centralised systems of which Sweden was one.

Thereafter, in the 1970s and 1980s, Lundgren and Mattsson identified rising concerns for two economic elements of the school system: its financial efficiency and its productivity. These factors grew in prominence as it became clear that merely investing in education was not producing the return to society at the level that human capital theory anticipated. The need for efficiency called for the decentralisation of financial management, while the need for productivity called for central direction in matters of school improvement, curriculum and attainment.

Lundgren and Mattsson (1996) were clear that decentralisation could not be a solution in itself; it had to be accompanied by certain types of action undertaken at the school level. The potential benefits of decentralisation were thus not only cost-effectiveness through better deployment of resources, but also the sharing of power, with its energising effects, and the development of a culture of learning at school level that would be expected to bring a local flavour to aspects of curriculum and pedagogy.

The spaces for school improvement under decentralisation might be found in the balances between central and local influences, and between political and professional influences. The top-down steering through legal, economic and ideological pressures, combined with evaluation systems, may be counter-balanced to a certain extent by certain kinds of school leadership (Lundgren and Mattsson, 1996). Caldwell (2008) presented important reflections on a commissioned study of how the concept of the self-managing school had evolved since the passage of the UK Education Reform Act, 20 years previously. The study was focused on England but incorporated inputs from 11 countries. Caldwell's perspective was also informed by his previous significant involvements in introducing structural change to school systems in Alberta and Victoria.

Caldwell (2008) challenged the critical stances, which had emphasised that the introduction of school autonomy had been politically motivated by a desire to privatise state education. While political papers, for example, Sexton (1977), had been written which did indeed overtly express that motive, it had not, in Caldwell's view, ever been pursued in practice in any of the key jurisdictions leading the school autonomy movement. Caldwell (2008) argued that critiques, which tied school-based management simplistically to the 'neo-liberal agenda', were not taking account of actual practice. He also cited the OECD (2008) report of its survey, which showed that many countries were de-centralising their school systems.

Caldwell (2008) observed that the original interest in the structural and financial management aspects of reform had evolved to incorporate greater interest in school-based leadership of learning. This interest had become significant by about the year 2000, and had increased since.

Caldwell (2008) argued that schools which had responded most successfully to autonomy and the focus on the leadership of learning were those that had developed four kinds of capital: intellectual, social, spiritual and financial. The ideas of developing intellectual and social capital are, of course, central to our interest in policy learning. In Caldwell's model, these four forms of capital were built through governance, and their combined effects improved the leadership of learning.

School Autonomy in Victoria, Australia

Boyd and Chapman (1987: 264) reviewed what they described as 'the most ambitious of the ventures now underway in Australia, that ongoing in the State of Victoria'. They attempted to identify the reasons for the Victorian exercise in decentralisation, devolution and school improvement, and the progress made at the time of their research.

Policies have push and pull factors: the 'push' of a perceived problem that needs to be solved, and the 'pull' of an attractive solution. Boyd and Chapman (1987) traced the history of the school system in Victoria, which had created in the nineteenth century a highly centralised Education Department, such that the school principals were in effect the local agents of the Department. They considered that this level of centralisation was excessive, and that it became a significant problem because of population growth and the rapid expansion of the school system. This led the Liberal government in 1975 to introduce a policy of decentralisation to create regional directorates and to grant increased autonomy to school principals. In its White Paper of 1980 the government elaborated its aims to localise administration; to encourage schools to take greater responsibility in education policy and curriculum; to give principals a greater say in the selection of teaching staff; and to increase the powers of School Councils (the equivalent of school governing bodies in England).

Boyd and Chapman (1987) noted that some commentators felt the plans for implementing this policy were such that they favoured efficiency over genuine participation. In 1982 Victoria had an incoming Labour government that greatly extended the policy, strengthening devolution of authority and responsibility at the school level, requiring collaborative decision-making processes, and emphasising effective educational outcomes including redressing disadvantage and discrimination.

Boyd and Chapman (1987) were clear about the link between this set of devolution policies and the school effectiveness movement. This had challenged the previous assumption that schools make little difference to educational outcomes, by identifying factors that made some schools unusually effective. These included the role of the principal in creating a strong sense of commitment among staff, and a strong sense of community. Seen through the lens suggested earlier, the Liberal policies were mainly seeking to adjust the institutional pattern to greatly increased scale because of population growth, whereas the Labour policies sought in addition to adjust the institutional pattern to new normative values; specifically, expectations about learner outcomes.

Boyd and Chapman (1987) reviewed the early stages of implementing the policy of devolution. They found very muted grassroots enthusiasm for such significant devolution among teachers and parents, its main drivers being Labour party intellectuals and state-level lobbyists. School principals felt that their decision-making powers had been reduced, not increased, because of the increased powers of School Councils and increased requirements to consult with staff and parents. Principals also reported that the change was rushed.

There are some notable points of contrast between the devolution policy in Victoria and its equivalent in England. In Victoria, the responsibilities of principals were to be increased at the same time as their responsibilities for administration; in England, the local management of schools coincided with the introduction of a National Curriculum restricting head teachers' freedoms. In Victoria, principals felt that their powers had been reduced, but in England the opposite happened. Head teachers were already accustomed to working with school governing bodies; most felt frustrations with aspects of administration by their local authorities and welcomed the opportunity to take control. The government's aim was to reduce the power and influence of local government, and it wanted to see head teachers becoming more important. The decision-making powers of head teachers in relation to school administration and management set off on a rising trajectory, which has continued to this day. Finally, devolution in England was phased, and supported by considerable investment and training.

School Autonomy in England

Any narrative of the increasing school autonomy in England needs to distinguish between autonomy in relation to curriculum and pedagogy on the one hand, and autonomy in relation to infrastructural management – finance, personnel and buildings – on the other. In the middle of the twentieth century, England had one of the most devolved school administration systems in the world. This constitution had been crafted by the generation who had fought fascism in Europe during the Second World War. In the words of William Picken Alexander,

> Let us therefore state at once the first principle and perhaps the most important principle on which the English system rests. We believe in the distribution of power. It has been said that the best safeguard for democracy is to ensure that a madman coming to power cannot ruin the people.... In England the power of the Minister is limited. The Education Act itself creates the local education authorities and governing bodies and determines in broad terms their respective functions, thus securing that power is appropriately distributed. (Alexander, 1954: 2–3)

Between the Education Act 1944 and the Education Reform Act 1988, these checks and balances applied, and in this period responsibility for the 'internal conduct, curriculum and discipline of the school' (i.e. curriculum and pedagogy) was compulsorily delegated by school governing bodies to head teachers. National government had strictly limited functions in relation to the curriculum, beyond the requirement of the Act that 'the curriculum shall promote the spiritual, moral, cultural, mental and physical wellbeing of pupils at school, and of society'. Thus head teachers had considerable autonomy in matters of curriculum and pedagogy, although a climate of consensus and tradition resulted in the learning experiences of pupils being broadly similar nationwide.

Local education authorities administered finance, personnel and buildings. The word 'leadership' was rarely used; functions in education were separated into policy, administration and practice. Nor, incidentally, was there much talk of 'attainment' except in relation to the top 25% of the ability range many of whom were, until the 1970s, educated in selective schools. This is the background against which the key policies of the Education Reform Act 1988 were introduced, comprising local management of schools, a national curriculum, and testing at ages 7, 11, 14 and 16. The combined effect of these policies was to reduce the autonomy of head teachers in relation to curriculum and pedagogy, and to increase their responsibilities for finance, personnel and buildings.

A national curriculum and testing were inevitable. During the oil crisis of the 1970s, in order to secure further advances from the International Monetary Fund, the then Prime Minister James Callaghan had needed to initiate a 'Great Debate' on the education of the future workforce with a view to making British industry more competitive. It was, however, the political choice of the Thatcher government that the National Curriculum would be dominated by the traditional academic curriculum of selective schools, rather than emphasising practical and vocational skills.

In the policy-making context of England the idea of what was termed 'local management of schools (LMS)', and elsewhere, 'site-based management', grew from an Alternative Use of Resources scheme developed by the (then) Inner London Education Authority; a fully developed LMS scheme pioneered by Cambridgeshire County Council in the mid-1980s; and it was also influenced by parallel developments taking place in the State of Victoria, Australia. Undoubtedly it appealed to the Thatcher government's sense of good housekeeping, and generally was warmly welcomed by schools. It is also necessary to acknowledge two other political motives: central government's hatred of local authorities, and hence its desire to clip their decision-making powers; and a desire to introduce market forces into state schooling. Along with other regulations regarding school admissions policies, Local Management of Schools provided a financial incentive for schools to compete for the number and quality of students admitted, thus creating 'winner' and 'loser' schools. It may surprise modern sensibilities that a national government would overtly and knowingly set out to create 'loser schools' within a universal public service.

Overall, the introduction and refinement of Local Management of Schools (subsequent amendments imposed more and more standardisation on school funding formulae, with decreasing discretion for local government) led to more efficient use of resources, and the provision of services to schools which were better suited to their needs. In most areas, new and better working relationships were forged between local authorities and their schools, reflecting increased transparency, partnership and shared decision-making. Nationwide, the overall effect of decisions by individual head teachers using their new financial freedom was to increase spending on teacher staffing and to economise on all other costs. The increased executive responsibilities of head teachers led many, especially of secondary schools, to re-invent themselves as 'chief executives' concentrating on the overall business success of their institutions, pushing down to lower levels the leadership of curriculum and pedagogy. There are lessons here for modern school systems seeking concurrently to promote both school autonomy and pedagogic progress.

A few years after the implementation of LMS, the national government set up the Office for Standards in Education (Ofsted) school inspection system. Ofsted's creation had not been planned; it was an opportunistic response to an amendment adopted during the passage of legislation that had been intended to produce significantly 'lighter touch' arrangements. The effect of Ofsted was to introduce a high-stakes inspection regime in which schools deemed not to meet its criteria were 'named and shamed', and suffered draconian intervention or were closed. Passing Ofsted inspection moved to the top of the priorities for most school leaders. Ofsted's views impinged on many aspects of the 'internal conduct, curriculum and discipline of the school'. So returning to the questions regarding leading what and leading how, by the end of the Conservative government in 1997, English school leaders were leading the business management of a school institution within a competitive market economy, and they were leading the 'delivery' of a nationally prescribed curriculum. That concerns 'what', but Ofsted inspection also affected 'how'. The threat of adverse judgement from Ofsted made it increasingly risky for head teachers to allow their professional judgement, philosophy, vision and values to stray too far from Ofsted's standard expectations. The autonomy over professional educational matters, which head teachers had enjoyed between 1944 and 1988, was finished.

Subsequent Policy Developments

When Tony Blair's New Labour government took office in June 1997, some education policies changed significantly, while others did not. The new government kept in place the academic curriculum and market mechanism of the previous government. The government's political advisers feared a harmful exodus from state schools to the independent sector, and wanted state schools to remain attractive to middle-class aspirational parents. To mitigate the effects of these inherited policies, the new government introduced a raft of new national programmes including improvements to early years education, and the national literacy and numeracy strategies. The latter two strategies were imposed across the nation, in cavalier disregard for constitutional conventions. Although there was no legal requirement on schools to implement the National Literacy

Strategy, packages of highly prescriptive teaching materials were delivered to every primary school, and only a very small number of schools were brave enough and had sufficient confidence in their own methods to refuse to use them. MacBeath (2008: 34) researched how head teachers in England talked about the National Strategies, and concluded that head teachers had needed to 'work out their own salvation', which had involved 'a quest for a marriage of convenience between dutiful compliance and intellectual subversion'.

In 2010, a new UK Conservative–Liberal Coalition government came to power, which changed the landscape significantly for autonomous schools. The government needed to reduce public spending, and had an ideological aversion to the scale of state interventionary activity the previous government had put in place. This took the form of numerous national educational agencies and quasi-autonomous bodies, with overlapping remits, and grant-funded teams of school improvement experts in local authorities. The latter device had neutralised local authorities as a tier of democratic government, making them mainly a convenient structure for national government's command and control system. The incoming government greatly reduced the scale both of the work of national agencies, and of the grant-funded support for local government, instead encouraging schools to leave local government by becoming 'academies' directly funded by central government. The return of a Conservative government in 2015 meant that these policy trends would continue.

Thus leaders of state schools in England have, regarding their legal powers, a very high level of autonomy in global terms. For some, 'more autonomy' simply means less support, with no reduction in accountability. There is an expectation that head teachers will collaborate to develop local infrastructures of mutual support. In some cases, 'successful' head teachers, as defined by the managerial, test-score-achieving, inspection-passing flavour of the times, are simply reproducing of their own volition the intimidating methods of working to which they have become conditioned. In other cases, the power vacuum left by the demise of effective local government has been filled by academy chains, led by philanthropists and entrepreneurial 'super-heads'. These structures may reduce the head teacher at an individual school to the status of a branch manager delivering the brand identity of the chain. It is too early to say whether and to what extent the extreme level of school autonomy in England will actually produce new professionally-led models of school improvement. It is interesting to juxtapose this crystallising pattern of school chains in England, with the many large chains of independent schools in South Asia, and in particular, India, which represent a significant sector of provision – one which influences perceptions of what is a quality education. Structures vary, but commonly principals of schools within these large independent chains do not have much local autonomy; most important decisions are taken by head office.

School Leadership Development Programmes in England

School leadership was addressed specifically by the Labour government (1997–2010), which passed legislation requiring head teachers of state schools to have a National Professional Qualification for Headship (NPQH). To implement this, the government established its own National College for School Leadership (NCSL) under its own tight control. The government had seen the significance of school leadership in a number of international settings, including the Australian State of Victoria (again), and the work of Vicki Phillips, then School District Superintendent in Philadelphia. To this genuine belief in the power of leadership might be added a further rationale, which may reasonably be inferred for this policy. While national government could not, by law and constitutional convention, take over the direct running of state schools (the legal conjuring trick of 'academies' had not yet been developed), it could come near to this by requiring every head teacher to be trained to think and behave in a certain way.

There were at the time a number of established and well-regarded university centres for school leadership. The establishment of NCSL attenuated these, but the new organisation had minimal capacity and expertise of its own, so designing the NPQH programme was contracted out and university school leadership centres made a significant contribution to the programme design. The delivery of the programme was also contracted out to a series of regional centres designated for the purpose. For example, the regional centre for Greater London was the (then) London Leadership Centre (later, the London Centre for Leadership in Learning) of the (then) Institute of Education, University of London. This centre had the monopoly responsibility for training every head teacher in London, and at its peak over 1000 candidates were passing through the programme at any one time. Such heavy involvement of university-based senior practitioner experts in the design, delivery and assessment of the programme ensured its quality. The NPQH programme emphasised practical application and skills development, and the programme and associated National Professional Standards for Headship, published in 2004, could for a time fairly be said to represent globally leading-edge practice. Certainly, they attracted enormous interest from visiting delegations from other countries.

Meanwhile, NCSL had expanded its remit well beyond the single statutory requirement for the NPQH. Around that statutory element, NCSL developed a range of additional programmes for each level of leadership on a typical career ladder, and programmes for other groups including school business managers (bursars). In addition to programmes, NCSL issued publications, held conferences, commissioned research, maintained a full and active website, and generally sought to position itself as the 'staff college' for school leaders. Its courses and activities were financially subsidised by government, and competed with and undercut those offered by university centres of school leadership. By these means, using Nye's (2012) 'soft power', the government through NCSL went a long way to co-opting an entire generation of school leaders into its ways of thinking.

The trajectory of NPQH did not remain at its zenith for more than a few years. It had become the professional development of choice for many senior staff in schools regardless of whether they intended to become head teachers, which did not accord with the Treasury's view of an efficient return on public investment. Admission to the programme was limited to those genuinely very close to achieving headship; the pattern of contracting was changed to limit the involvement that any single provider could have, and the programme itself was re-fashioned from a structured course of learning to a competence-proving, evidence-gathering model.

A further change reflected New Labour's style of governing. The government had initiated a complex array of policy implementation programmes across education and related children's services, and had established or expanded a large number of different, yet overlapping, national agencies charged with driving the implementation of these programmes. As one expression of the government's love of top-down micro-management, the practice developed that each of the government's programmes should incorporate elements to reinforce the implementation of all the other related programmes. Thus NPQH suffered subtle but noticeable changes in flavour, slightly away from the central concerns of how to run a school, and slightly more towards ensuring that participants understood and were committed to supporting a raft of political priorities and topical fixations.

Brundrett et al. (2006) had critiqued national programmes of school leadership development both in England and New Zealand, considering that in both cases they had been designed to create orthodoxy and compliance to centrally mandated norms. They argued that fundamental questions about the nature of school leadership and its knowledge base should be re-surfaced, which, in the case of New Zealand, had by 2013 to some extent occurred (see next section).

School Leadership Development Worldwide

With the additional responsibilities of school autonomy, especially where these became combined with high-pressure accountability, school principals needed to develop their leadership skills in ways relevant to these specific challenges. Some forms of development were planned by governments, but much also depended on self-help strategies. In relation to Victoria, Boyd and Chapman (1987) noted that principals had reported to them that there had been a serious lack of training for their new role, and a lack of sufficient financial resources; they were just told to 'get on with it'. They did not feel that they had been adequately involved in the design and implementation of the change.

Boyd and Chapman (1987: 264–5) concluded that the reform effort had brought about 'a tremendous change in the ... content and semantics of discourse about school administration and school-community relations', but that

> (t)he implementation of the plan has suffered from a neglect of the retraining and in-service activities needed to facilitate learning the new attitudes and roles fundamental to the new style of collaborative management which was mandated. (Boyd and Chapman, 1987: 264)

MacBeath et al. (2012) researched the 'coping strategies' of Scottish school principals, and classified these as 'dutiful compliance', 'cautious pragmatism', 'quiet self-confidence', 'bullish self-assertion' and 'defiant risk-taking' – designations which capture both the human element and the developmental challenges for principals.

In New Zealand, a country noted for the extent to which decision-making was devolved to the school level, Cardno and Youngs (2013) reported on their evaluation of the Experienced Principals' Development programme (EPDP). This programme had been developed specifically to provide appropriate forms of learning to revitalise and re-enthuse experienced principals, in ways that would offer individualised approaches to development. Cardno and Youngs (2013) judged EPDP to be successful in this regard, especially by offering coaching and mentoring within credible, trustworthy relationships; reflection and problem-solving experiences requiring an extensive repertoire of problem-relevant knowledge; professional renewal through intellectual challenge and increased emotional intelligence; and direct involvement in school-based enquiry projects and action research.

Some pre-service development programmes for principals were reviewed by Walker et al. (2013). These included the Ontario Principals Qualification Programme, the State of Victoria Master of School Leadership (Australia), the Singapore Leaders in Education programme, the New York City Aspiring Principals Programme, and the Hong Kong Certificate for Principalship. Although each of these programmes was distinctive, they also had significant elements in common, regarding both the knowledge base and the methods of learning. In particular, frequent use of practical application projects such as action research, mentoring, internships, and the compilation of a journal or portfolio featured in these programmes (Walker et al., 2013). These programmes were predicated on a culture of decentralisation and school principal autonomy. It is interesting to contrast this pattern with the position in Mainland China where the school system, whatever its other merits, remains highly authoritarian. There, Shuangye and Zheng (2014) reviewed policy for developing principals between 1989 and 2011, and found that the dominant feature of this provision was the extreme level of state control over every aspect of the design, participation in, and conduct of these programmes.

In most fully developed school systems, the leadership standards which inform, and are informed by, leadership development activity for school principals assume that principals are engaged in much the same kind of work throughout the jurisdiction. In systems that are not fully developed, this assumption cannot be made. On the contrary, principals will be working in contrasting contexts; often, the less developed the system, then the wider the material and infrastructural disparities between the elite schools and those serving the most disadvantaged communities. In elite contexts, with highly motivated students, high resources and high expectations, the central role for the principal may be the cultivation of excellence. In contexts of specialised intervention, where students present complex needs but where infrastructural support is strong, the core role of the principal may be as a technician and expert problem-solver. Other principals work in contexts of high student motivation, but with very few resources, where the students themselves are the main available resource: here, the main role of the principal may be as the transformer who unlocks the latent energy of the students to build and develop the school. Some principals work in contexts of the most extreme challenge, in the absence either of resources or motivation to learn, in settings created by displacements, conflicts and natural disasters. Here, the role of the principal may combine being a humanitarian relief worker, an initiator of structures, and a purveyor of hope. Principals in all of these settings have something to learn from each other. Governments considering national schemes for school leadership development need to be cognisant of the true range of contexts within their jurisdiction.

Decentralised Schools in Contemporary Contexts

Governments currently considering the significant restructuring of their school system, and wishing to have regard to some of the lessons learnt in systems that pioneered such restructurings, need to be aware of how many factors have changed since the 1980s. Current understandings of quality assurance, equity and accountability mean that all jurisdictions are likely to want to balance institutional autonomy with centrally directed systems for standardisation and improvement. International comparisons, especially the OECD's PISA analysis, are reinforcing that trend.

Another change is, simply, the pace of change since the 1980s. It is easy to forget that one of the English categories of autonomous school, the 'grant maintained school', was invented by the Thatcher government not to stimulate change but to shield schools from change. This category was intended to offer an escape route for schools to 'opt out' of so-called 'loony left' local authorities ('loony' because of their interest in countering discrimination on the grounds of race, gender and disability). The policy backfired badly, but the point is that autonomy can just as well enable fossilisation as progress. In most modern school systems, institutional 'freedom' will come with a non-negotiable reform agenda. Many developing systems are working within planning frameworks which assume that they will be able to deliver in, perhaps five or ten years, a level of reform equivalent to that which took 30 or 40 years in England. Unpredictability of funding also affects the extent to which it is helpful to delegate financial management to schools. This presupposes financial planning and good housekeeping over a period. In some developing systems, school funding is dominated by short-term donor-related schemes.

The concepts of spatiality can throw additional light on matters of education policy, management and practice. This line of argument builds on the ideas of Taylor (2011) and Gulson (2005) on education geography; Yi-Fu Tuan (1996) and Rigg (2007) on the nature and making of spaces; and Urry (2007) on mobility.

The world that school leaders inhabit is made up of places, spaces, networks and mobilities. 'Places' are physical locations that have their own distinctive and influential qualities. 'Spaces' describes the subjective experience of places and the associations attached to them by the various actors who use them (or who are excluded from them). 'Networks' describes an individual's connectedness to, and relationships within, patterns both of human contacts and materialities, the latter including ideas, cultures and institutions. 'Mobilities' describes meaningful movements from one place to another, as well as 'journeys' of an intellectual or cultural nature.

For most school leaders, the school campus and its local geographical context defines the 'place' where they work. While much can in fact be done over time to alter the characteristics of 'place', in the short term they are effectively a fixed factor. By contrast, 'spaces' not only reflect the diverse perspectives of individuals, but may also change profoundly for better or worse, and can do so quickly and frequently. Events and relationships, especially power dynamics, impact on people's spaces. How those impacts are dealt with (if they are negative) and utilised (if they are positive) will reflect an individual's dispositions, but it is often also the case that the nature of an individual's networks and mobilities has a direct bearing on their capacity to make the best of their spaces. The social nature of schools means that space-making by a school leader impacts on the space-making of others. Overall, however, it is reasonable to assert that while places are fixed in the short term, individuals either already have, or can be enabled to assert, a certain amount of agency and choice regarding their spaces, networks and mobilities.

This chapter is concerned with whether and to what extent the process of school autonomy will impact positively on the spaces in which school principals work; and this in turn depends on how it will enhance their networks, mobilities and sense of agency. If school principals' contexts are seen as particular combinations of places, spaces, networks and mobilities, then a further step is to see these through three different lenses: as intended by power-holders and opinion-formers; as lived and experienced by participants; and as objectively observed. These distinctions derive from Lefebvre (1991), who applied to them the confusing terms, respectively, of representations of space, spaces of representation and spatial practice.

Robertson (2009) applied this thinking to school decentralisation in England. She saw the spaces as intended by planners operating through discourses of choice, markets, self-management, entrepreneurialism, local visioning, sub-contracting, public–private partnerships, social capital and community expertise. Spaces as experienced included perceptions of consumerism, anxiety about responsibility for the future, different feelings of involvement, organisational responsibility without power, performativity and surveillance. Spatial practice included movements of responsibility to new nodes, different geometries of governance, and competitiveness (Roberston, 2009), to which might be added a high proportion of teachers leaving the profession within the first five years.

Many systems are becoming interested in teacher professionalisation. This involves the taking of responsibility not only collectively by the profession as a whole, but also by each practitioner, in patterns that cut across the organisational pattern of autonomous schools. Professionalisation implies that teachers assert an enhanced sense of ownership over the spaces they occupy; and that spaces of prescription become spaces of negotiation. This transition will be supported by significantly increased engagement in professional networks external to the workplace, and by independent external recognition of professional achievements, which should enhance mobility and career development choices.

Governments themselves sometimes find it more efficacious to work with individual practitioners rather than with institutions. This particularly applies in the context of developing systems where there are profound inadequacies in the capacities of the schools, and where the improvement strategy may involve especially selected and trained cadres of change agents to impact on the system in particular ways. This tactic is also found in mature systems. For example it formed a significant part of the UK Labour government's National Literacy Strategy. A very similar model was developed in Colombia to deploy specialists who would work alongside teachers to improve the teaching of language and maths.

A system designing a package of school reform must ask itself where, in order of priority, school autonomy should be placed. Often prior attention has to be given to developing communications infrastructures, and raising the capacity of school-based personnel, including leaders, to the point where they can use autonomy wisely. It is easy for Western commentators to over-estimate the capacity present in developing systems. In England, before the local management of schools, government agencies never made direct provision of a range of services that are routinely provided by Ministries of Education in developing systems: arranging for the authoring, printing and distribution of textbooks, for the manufacture and distribution of school furniture, for the setting, printing and marking of all examinations, and so on. Often there are no alternative sources of supply, and the majority of Ministry personnel are occupied with these 'nuts and bolts' rather than with strategic governance. Whether the necessary level of growth in capacity is achieved through a process of professionalisation, or through some other form of intensive development of teaching cadre, such change is likely to have profound implications for schools as organisations.

Etzioni's (1961) classic work on congruent compliance structures identified three kinds of power – coercive, remunerative and normative – and three kinds of involvement by organisation members – alienative, calculative and moral – and that compliance structures were congruent when paired in the order stated. The different congruent compliance structures are appropriate to different organisations: normative–moral might apply to a church or a university, while coercive–alienative might be found in a prison. Often, however, different compliance patterns occur at different levels within an organisation, for example, for leadership it may be normative–moral, for middle managers it may be remunerative–calculative, and for the lowest level of operatives it may be coercive–alienative. Compliance structures may differ between what is officially intended, and what is perceived by various actors. Thus, organisational characteristics link to the spatial distinction between spaces as intended by planners, as objectively observed, and as experienced by those involved. A stronger sense of agency by teachers is bound to affect the nature of compliance structures in schools.

Classic theories of organisations use different explanatory analogies. There has been a recent resurgence, especially in the language of 'school-to-school support', in the personification of schools; schools take decisions and collaborate in certain ways, as if schools were sentient persons, as if schools were not composed of people with minds of their own. As school systems become more mature, perhaps schools will be less like mechanical systems (Easton, 1979) or living organisms (Silverman, 1971), and have more of the granular, individualised features identified in Greenfield's (1975) phenomenological model. Reed's (1992) notion of the postmodern organisation may also be relevant. This is characterised by network structures, informal divisions of labour, high-trust work relations, participative decision-making, and advanced use of ICT.

The critical literature on school autonomy (see for example, Smyth, 1993) noted that as autonomy (accountability) for managing money, buildings and people increased, autonomy decreased in relation to core educational matters such as curriculum, pedagogy and assessment, which became increasingly subject to political whim. Professionalisation can reclaim some of that territory in old systems and achieve greater balance from the outset in newly developing systems, with this increased agency manifesting itself not only at institutional level, but also at profession-wide level and at the level of individual practitioners. Thus, school autonomy, an essentially administrative and market-driven notion, will be counterbalanced by the (non-institution focused) notion of professional autonomy, concerning the heart of educational practice.

Perspectives on Reform

Levin and Fullan (2008) reviewed the lessons that had been learnt about effective school system reform, focusing primarily on England in the period since the passage of the Education Reform Act 1988, whilst drawing relevant international comparisons. They considered that the English reform was 'stronger, bigger, bolder' (ibid.: 290) than equivalent reforms that had slightly preceded it in New Zealand and in several states and districts of the USA. This applied particularly to the belief behind the English reforms that competition between schools would lead to school improvement: they noted that few other jurisdictions adopted this aim to the same extent.

Levin and Fullan (2008: 291) proposed a number of learning points arising from their review of the reform, including:

> Large scale, sustained improvement in student outcomes requires a sustained effort to change school and classroom practices, not just structures such as governance and accountability. The heart of improvement lies in changing teaching and learning practices in thousands and thousands of classrooms, and this requires focused and sustained effort by all parts of the education system and its partners.

Levin and Fullan (2008: 296) note that '(m)ost change efforts are weak on capacity building, and that is one of the key reasons why they fall short'. They define 'capacity building' somewhat prescriptively as 'any strategy that increases the collective effectiveness of a group to raise the bar and close the gap of student learning' (ibid.: 295).

Levin and Fullan's (2008: 292–3) analysis identified seven factors for successful large-scale change: a small number of ambitious yet achievable goals, publicly stated; a positive stance with a focus on motivation; multi-level engagement with strong leadership and a 'guiding coalition'; an emphasis on capacity building, with a focus on results; keeping a focus on key strategies while also managing other interests and issues; the effective use of resources; and the maintenance of a constant and growing transparency including public and stakeholder communication and feedback. In elaboration of 'strong leadership', Levin and Fullan (2008: 294) considered that '(t)here can be – indeed there should be – room for a variety of strategies to achieve the goals, but there cannot be substantial dissent on the main purposes themselves'. When this approach is combined with their desire to exchange top-down change to structures, for top-down change to practice in 'thousands of classrooms', it begins to look very similar to 'deliverology' as practised and refined by Michael Barber (Barber et al., 2011). That such approaches, deploying sophisticated forms of power and persuasion, can 'deliver' the outcomes that their instigators want is not in doubt. They do, however, seriously diminish the concepts of school autonomy and school leadership: in a command-and-control structure, 'autonomy' becomes the codeword for accountability, and 'leadership' becomes the codeword for the obedient implementation of orders.

There is, therefore, a clear tension between any meaningful understanding of school autonomy, and the advocacy of change strategies that depend on micro-managerial interference in that autonomy. The changes that flow from 'deliverology' require standardisation, whereas increasing school autonomy requires acceptance of increased diversity. There are two ways in which the tensions might be reduced between the benefits of real school autonomy and real school leadership, on the one hand, and the lessons of effective change management, as researched by experts, on the other hand. First, to adjust the timescales and specificity of the changes that central jurisdictions wish to mandate, making them longer term, more strategic, of a higher order and capable of being realised in a variety of different ways. Secondly, to localise the mechanisms that support change management, enabling local ownership and accepting that different localities will use their autonomy to adopt different approaches.

Decentralisation and School Autonomy in Bihar

Our exploration of decentralisation and school autonomy, principally as it has played out in two very important jurisdictions – Victoria, Australia and England – has identified a range of challenges complicating the implementation of these policies. In summary, the two key challenges are harmoniously orchestrating changing roles and the development of skills and capacities to exercise those roles; and protecting the core intentions of these policies from the counteracting effects of other concurrent policies, such as top-down standardisations in accountability and curriculum. Next we consider the same issues as they relate to India and the Indian states, taking Bihar as an example. One of the 29 states of India, it has an inadequate educational infrastructure creating a huge mismatch between demand and supply. As one of the 'heartland' states, Bihar was impacted differently from the 'rimland' states by nineteenth-century colonial development. In particular, the level and pace of economic development was lower, and the spread of English models of education took place later and to a lesser degree. These historical differences had a lasting negative impact on Bihar's level of prosperity and on the capacity of its administrative infrastructure. This problem is further compounded by increases in population. The craving for higher education among the general population of Bihar has led to a migration of the student community from the state. This in turn has led to a 'flooding' of students to seek educational opportunities in other states, even for graduation level college education. The schooling system in Bihar is largely as it was during the British rule.

Data for the years 2003–04 from the National Institute of Educational Planning and Administration revealed that 96.5% of Bihar's primary schools lack toilets for girls, and 20% of schools do not have a blackboard. Of Bihar's teachers 37.8% could not be found during unannounced visits to schools – the worst teacher absence rate in India and one of the worst in the world. A recent survey by NUEPA has determined that only 21% of all primary school teachers in Bihar have completed the matriculation, or 10th standard. Thus in terms of school effectiveness, the state schools in Bihar show obvious deficiencies, and it is noteworthy that all well-publicised examples of improvements in school effectiveness have been achieved through strong external interventions, and none through decentralisation and school autonomy on their own.

The state government administers state schools in Bihar and these state schools are affiliated with the Bihar School Examination Board. There is also a system of District Schools called Zilla Schools. There are a large number of schools affiliated with the Central Board of Secondary Education (CBSE) and the Council for Indian School Certificate Examination (CICSE). These schools include Convent Schools, Kendriya Vidyalayas, and Jawahar Navodaya Vidyalayas. In the post-liberalisation era the number of private schools, including school-chains and Missionary Schools run by Christian Missionaries as well as Madarsas, or schools run by Muslim clerics, has increased. The school-chains and Missionary Schools run by Christian Missionaries are considered as some of the best schools in the state. This diversity in the pattern of school governance and sources of accreditation, combined with the low positioning of state schools in the perceived quality hierarchy, adds to the difficulties of attempting systemic change through initiatives focused on the state schools.

The literacy rate in Bihar is low as there is a huge gap between demand and supply for school education as well as for higher education. The state requires more schools and institutes for higher education. Most of the schools in Bihar are affiliated with the Bihar School Examination Board, while the Kendriya Vidyalayas and a few other elite schools including the Christian Missionary Schools are affiliated to the CICSE and CBSE boards.

In line with the National Policy of Education (NPE) launched in 1986 and the Programme of Action (POA) launched in 1992 a number of schemes and programmes were introduced in Bihar. These included Operation Blackboard (OBB); Non Formal Education (NFE); Teacher Education (TE); Mahila Samakhya (MS); the National Programme of Nutritional Support to Primary Education (MDM); the District Primary Education Program (DPEP); the UNICEF supported programmes run by SPEED; and finally the Sarva Shiksha Abhiyan (SSA).

Sarva Shiksha Abhiyan was a response to the demand for quality basic education through a system of decentralised planning and management (a goal set by the NPE in 1986) and direct community involvement provided by the 73rd and 74th constitutional amendments, which facilitated the transfer of power, participation and effective involvement of the local self-government institutions – Panchayat Raj Institutions (PRIs), School Management Committees (SMCs), Village and Urban Slum Level Education Committees (VECs), Parent Teacher Associations (PTAs), Mother Teacher Associations (MTAs), Tribal Autonomous Councils and other grassroot level structures – in the management of elementary schools. At the village level, a Village Education Committee had the principal responsibility for community mobilisation, school mapping, micro planning, renovation and construction of school buildings and improvements to the pedagogical curriculum. In terms of Lauglo's (1996) models of decentralisation, these policies seem to rely heavily on populist localism, with elements of deconcentration (bringing elements of accountability in closer geographical proximity to the school), without the necessary attention being paid to building the capacity of school principals and other senior professionals to meet these expectations.

As we suggested in Chapter 2, Sarva Shiksha Abhiyan (SSA) is the government of India's flagship programme for the achievement of the Universalisation of Elementary Education (UEE) in a time bound manner, as mandated by the 86th amendment to the Constitution of India, making free and compulsory education to the children of 6–14 years age group a fundamental right. SSA is being implemented in partnership with state governments to cover the entire country and address the needs of 192 million children in 1.1 million habitations. The programme seeks to open new schools in those habitations which do not have schooling facilities and strengthen existing school infrastructure through the provision of additional classrooms, toilets, drinking water, maintenance grants and school improvement grants. Existing schools with inadequate teacher strength are provided with additional teachers, while the capacity of existing teachers is being strengthened by extensive training, grants for developing teaching-learning materials and the strengthening of the academic support structure at a cluster, block and district level. Sarva Shiksha Abhiyan seeks to provide quality elementary education including life skills, and it has a special focus on girls' education and children with special needs. It also seeks to provide computer education to bridge the digital divide.

The thrust of these policies, driven by a desire for the equitable inclusion in learning of marginalised or disadvantaged groups, is to direct specific initiatives to each of these prioritised needs. India is by no means alone in selecting this strategy, but in a context where provision in the mainstream is seriously inadequate, global experience can also be seen to support the view that improving education in the mainstream is actually essential to making very much progress in improving education for marginalised groups.

Sarva Shiksha Abhiyan allowed states to formulate context specific guidelines within the overall framework, to encourage districts to reflect local specificity; and to promote local need-based planning based on broad national policy norms. The emphasis was on mainstreaming out-of-school children through diverse strategies, and on providing eight years of schooling for all children in the 6–14 age groups. The core of the policy was on the bridging of gender and social gaps and a total retention of all children in schools. Within this framework it was expected that the education system would be made relevant so that children and parents find the schooling system useful and absorbing, according to their natural and social environments. The objectives were expressed nationally though it was expected that various states and districts were likely to achieve universalisation in their own respective contexts and in their own time frame.

A range of issues and strategies to promote decentralised management and community ownership was part of Sarva Shiksha Abhiyan. These can be categorised as institutional, financial, community ownership, sustainable support, capacity building, administrative, community-based monitoring, habituation planning, girls' education and special needs.

With the first of these, the state was required to make an objective review and assessment of the various components of the education system including educational administration, financial issues, decentralisation and community ownership, recruitment of teachers, monitoring and evaluation, status of the education of girls, SC/ST and disadvantaged groups, policy regarding private schools and ECCE, and undertake reforms in order to improve the efficiency of the delivery system. With the second there was a desire to develop a long-term perspective on the financial partnership between the Central and the State governments to make elementary education interventions sustainable.

The third strategy was community ownership of school-based interventions through effective decentralisation, augmented by involvement of women's groups, VSS and PRI members and other grassroots organisations. However, without a major capacity-building exercise involving national, state and district level institutions, these school-based interventions were fragile initiatives. There was also a need to improve the administration of schools through institutional development, the infusion of new approaches and by the adoption of cost effective and efficient methods.

A fourth strategy adopted by Bihar State was to develop sustainable support systems of resources for all the people in the system and the institutions. And a fifth strategy was community-based monitoring with full transparency, and to this end they adopted a new educational management information system (EMIS) to correlate school level data with community-based information from micro planning and surveys. Besides this, every school was to be encouraged to share all their information with the community. Habituation plans were designated as the basis for formulating district plans. The overarching principle was accountability to the community. However, within this, priority was to be given to the education of girls and to the inclusion and participation of children from scheduled castes and scheduled tribes, minority groups, urban deprived children, disadvantaged groups and children with special needs, in the educational process. This suite of strategies illustrates both the blurred distinctions between decentralisation that empowers people and decentralisation which gives responsibilities to people, which is beyond their capacities; and also forms of decentralisation which are fundamentally disempowering for the local professional leaders of education.

While the overall framework of SSA (as detailed above) provided for decentralisation, specific guidelines for school level decentralised management were missing. Norms and rules were spread across different components of SSA, for example, norms for community mobilisation included those for enrolment/supervision of localised repair of schools, practices for the functioning of VECs, for the provision of support in managing school functioning and the arrangement of mid-day meals. However, academic monitoring was centralised or top-down; there appeared to be very little scope for bottom-up processes to take effect. It was a case of centralised decentralisation; people were told at different levels what they could do, but agency connecting it to the ground was missing. The vagueness of guidelines meant that different states interpreted it in their own way, leading to tremendous variation.

Complementarity and Mutuality

Actors at all levels of governance and leadership need to develop a shared understanding of how their roles interact in order to generate systemic coherence whilst supporting beneficial learning at all levels. This is likely to embrace the principle of subsidiarity, with high level policy concentrating on broad, long-term strategic aims; issues of entitlement and equity; and structural policies in relation to accountability and quality assurance. The principle of complementarity aims to achieve effective teamwork, where actors at different levels and of different kinds are enabled to make additions to the value chain which draw most appropriately on their technical and contextual knowledge, and on their ability to make things happen. The principle of mutuality recognises the interdependence of individuals and units in a devolved system. Patterns of cooperation and collaboration are essential and these cut across hierarchical structures. For example, if front-line practitioners want to be well led and well governed, they must understand the needs of actors at different levels and be proactive in feeding them with information and ideas. Mutuality might be represented by the relationships between kite, string and wind. The kite of systemic policy and leadership would fall down if not braced by the string connecting it to practice, and the wind in this analogy represents the thrust of global, national and local aspiration.

The third productive practice we identified in Chapter 1 and now take up at a deeper level in the next chapter refers to removing barriers to inclusive education. This reform concentrated on India's efforts to improve educational and social outcomes for all their students. Particular attention was paid to inclusive education reform initiatives that allowed the inclusion of vulnerable students such as indigenous students, and policies and programmes that dealt with a range of issues of student displacement through poverty, family migration, the education of refugee children and the girl child. Also foregrounded were recent approaches to the education of children with disabilities.

6

INCLUSIVE PRACTICES

This chapter explores the implications of recent education policy developments for inclusive education. Given that globalising education policy expresses an ethic of competitive individualism (cf. Rizvi and Lingard, 2010), our concern here is with issues of diversity and exclusion in a globalising education context, and from this a framework for inclusive education can be developed. This framework for inclusion is built from particular understandings of governance and accountability arrangements, professionalism and resilience, localised reforms and relationships between learning opportunities and the community.

It allows us to identify important elements of inclusive education. Any framework for inclusion is founded upon a comprehensive understanding of the local context and the specific dynamics of inclusion and exclusion. This discussion draws on international literature to provide examples of dismantling barriers to educational access, participation and success (for example, Slee, 2010; Booth and Ainscow, 2011). Reflecting on the OECD review of education for migrant and disadvantaged populations (OECD, 2010b) in various social contexts enables us to examine contested policy approaches and consider approaches to inclusion across a range of educational and cultural contexts. We conclude the chapter with a discussion of building schools as communities by identifying important linkages across and within major social institutions. Central to the aspirations of reform is an adherence to the principles of inclusion and justice. Consequently, community and family engagement are at the heart of reforming education. In considering questions of the mitigation of the effects of shifting and displaced populations, the educational status of the girl child, education for scheduled castes, indigenous children, children living in extreme economic deprivation and disabled children, are fundamental problems that education reformers in India are attempting to respond to. This chapter suggests ways of developing more inclusive educational and social responses to exclusion.

Understanding Diversity and Exclusion

Inclusive education is broadly 'understood as a reform that supports and welcomes diversity amongst all learners' (UNESCO, 2009: 8). The diversity of learners and thus their differences is understood in a broad sense within the inclusive education discourse and it refers to such matters as ability or dis-ability, ethnic origin, religion, sexual orientation, race, gender and economic class (UNESCO, 2009). Further to this, inclusive education points to an amelioration or betterment of the effects of discrimination by the school and the whole society, directed towards accepting, representing and celebrating differences. This also caters for and addresses the individual needs of students in order to tackle their educational as well as their social exclusion (UNESCO, 2009). The transformation of the (inclusive) school is understood as a constant process within the inclusive education discourse.

It is important to understand that the discourse of inclusive education is not always a reliable indicator of inclusive educational practice. Education jurisdictions around the world have readily adopted the language of inclusion while maintaining assumptions about the nature of student differences and academic achievement that maintain the educational architecture of exclusion. Here we refer to the commonplace substitution of the discourse of inclusion to describe traditional beliefs and practices of special education (Brantlinger, 2006). Such beliefs limit opportunities and achievement, as Black-Hawkins et al. (2007) and Rix (2015) suggest. Bauman (2004) contends that although the discourse of inclusion is now ubiquitous, it conceals an abiding 'mixaphobia' or fear of difference.

Inclusive education has become an important priority for both political and educational systems worldwide. For example, it is included in the Europe 2020 policy agenda, under the heading of 'Promoting Equity, Social Cohesions and Active Citizenship' and in national inclusion statements such as the following:

> all Australian governments and all school sectors must provide all students with access to high-quality schooling that is free from discrimination based on gender, language, sexual orientation, pregnancy, culture, ethnicity, religion, health or disability, socioeconomic background or geographic location. (Ministerial Council on Education, 2008: 7)

Inclusive education draws on a number of old and well established social and political values, such as safeguarding and promoting social inclusion, equal opportunities, human rights, social justice, social respect, participation, achievement, diversity and solidarity (UNESCO, 2009). Furthermore, it is legitimised through a number of legal frameworks, both older and well established as well as more recent ones, including the 1979 Convention on the Elimination of All Forms of Discrimination against Women; the 1989 Convention on the Rights of the Child; the 2005 Convention on the Protection and Promotion of Diversity in Cultural Expressions; and the 2006 Convention on the Rights of Persons with Disabilities. These international conventions are instantiated in local anti-discrimination and equal opportunity legislation (Norwich, 2013).

Inclusive education has historically developed from the notions of 'integration' and 'special education' (Graham and Slee, 2008). During the 1970s, the influential Warnock report in the United Kingdom (Warnock Committee, 1978) described the placing of 'children with special needs' in segregated schools as an exclusionary practice. Further to this, she emphasised the urgent need for children to be integrated in mainstream schools in order to overcome their physical marginalisation by placing them alongside their peers and by offering them a special educational needs (SEN) programme. From this standpoint, integration came to be opposed to the notion of segregation (Norwich, 2013). However, the integration agenda has been criticised for disregarding the differences between people and for assuming that children should be acculturated and assimilated into an already existing, stable and fixed educational system (see, for example, Barton, 2005; Slee, 2008).

During the 1990s there was a heated debate about the new notion of inclusive education and how it could address integration. The stigma of the integration–inclusion difference debate is illustrated in the following metaphor: '(w)hilst integration was the square peg struggling to fit the round holes, inclusion is a circle containing many different shapes and sizes, all interrelating into the whole' (Corbett and Slee, 2000: 140). This points to a variety of inclusion characteristics, namely the acceptance and celebration of students' differences, and the need to change and transform both the school as well as the wider educational and social system. This is also relevant to the inclusive education idea of diverting the emphasis away from 'seeing the child as the problem to seeing the education system as the problem' (UNESCO, 2009: 14).

The underpinning philosophy of inclusive education systems has in the past drawn on two dominant and contradictory models of disability, namely the medical and social models. Generally, advocates of special education and integration are considered to support the medical model, while purists of inclusion favour the social model of disability. While the medical/charity model suggests that problems and differences lie with the individual (WHO, 2011), the social model places the emphasis on socio-economic and cultural factors (cf. Oliver, 1996).

Examples of socio-economic factors are poor nutrition or contaminated water (Barnes and Mercer, 2005), while cultural factors refer to the ideological construction of the notion of disability or difference. For example, the language used in a specific culture for disability or disadvantage indicates what is considered to be normal or abnormal in that culture. From this perspective, the focus of the medical model is on biology, which points to a physical treatment for disability and difference. In contrast, in adopting a social model, the emphasis is placed on social barriers to inclusion, such as place ramps in the streets to help people with disabilities move around. Additionally, from a cultural point of view, the emphasis is on the need to transform the attitudes adopted in relation to, and the language used about, disability and difference, because it impacts on how well people with disabilities or differences can be successfully included and represented in society (Eskay et al., 2012).

In a critique of the dominant models of disability (i.e. medical, socio-economic, cultural) Bhaskar and Danermark (2006: 281) argue that 'each of these models accentuates just one of what are in fact a multiplicity of mechanisms involved in the formation and reproduction of disabilities'. For instance, the social model has omitted the 'disabled body' from the discourse (Allan, 2008) by shifting the emphasis from the biological to the environmental (Graham and Slee, 2008). And the medical model, in turn, has neglected environmental factors by foregrounding the 'disabled body'. Recent research on disability encourages a more holistic approach and emphasises all the different levels of reality (see Titchkosky, 2007; Shakespeare, 2014). For Rouse and Florian (1997), inclusive education is a socio-economic, political and cultural matter. This approach is supported by the World Health Organisation's definition of inclusion that adopts a 'bio-psycho-social' model of disability (WHO, 2011).

Inclusive Reform Agendas

Reform agendas, however well-intentioned, have the potential to either attenuate or exacerbate social disparities and exclusions. For example, we need to accept the potential for ICT-based initiatives to have a gap widening effect in the absence of significant investment in disadvantaged and remote communities. Russell Bishop and his colleagues (2010: 46) argue that policy measures for universal education have failed to produce equitable outcomes and have, in addition, enhanced the dominance of majority cultures:

> [...] educational reform that focuses on all students actually maintains the status quo of educational disparities, because any innovation tends to focus on how it can benefit children of the majority culture more than how it can benefit children of minority cultures. An associated problem is that initiatives that promote the social production of the majority culture often reinforce notion of deficiency that majority-culture teachers have about minority-culture children.

Schools, research tells us, are powerful agents of social exclusion (cf. Wilkinson and Pickett, 2009; Dorling, 2010) and this research is long-standing and extensive. The development of what was then called the 'new sociology of education' (Bowles and Gintis, 1976, for example) investigated the ways in which the school curriculum was founded upon and reinforced the cultural attributes of children from class elites (Bourdieu and Passeron, 1977). As a result, children from privileged families successfully completed school and their transmission into higher education and professional work was typically seamless. This was not the case for working class children who were failed by school. They left school before completing their education and found their place in the semi-skilled and unskilled labour market. Immigrant children, indigenous children, children living in isolated communities and disabled children were amongst those who have also experienced forms of educational exclusion (Slee, 2010).

Sadly, this research has not been made redundant by history. Researchers such as Willms (2003) in Canada, Teese and Polesel (2003) in Australia, Kozol (2005) in America, and Dorling (2010) and Wilkinson and Pickett (2009) in the United Kingdom depict growing disparities in the educational outcomes for children to the disadvantage of economically deprived families. Stephen Ball (1990, 1994, 2007 and 2008) is amongst a number of researchers who have demonstrated the pernicious effects of education policies on groups of disadvantaged students. League tables and high stakes testing programmes around the world have in addition had the effect of inducing schools to exclude students whose educational prospects looked to be weak and would therefore reflect badly on school inspection reports and league table positions (Gillborn and Youdell, 2000).

As the pressure for competition between schools (through targets and league tables) and indeed countries (through PISA and other international rankings) increases, special education becomes a convenient mechanism to exclude underperforming and difficult students. Moreover, according to a review of labour market statistics (Slee, 2010), those who participated in segregated special education are disadvantaged when compared with disabled children who are educated in their neighbourhood school, when seeking work in the paid job market, thereby leading to long-term social exclusion. Researchers such as Linda Graham and her colleagues in Sydney are extending this research to consider the relationship between the assignment of children to special educational needs categories and incarceration (Graham et al., 2014).

An example of a more inclusive education policy is the Finnish system. As a result of its strong welfare state that supports the education system and economic stability, public education is provided free as a universal and constitutional right. Finnish schools are considered as focal centres for their communities. Regardless of students' social class, schools provide the necessary resources and free hot meals, as well as health and dental services, psychological counselling and a broad array of other services for students and their families (Pearson Foundation, 2011).

A low student–teacher ratio enables teachers to maximise the learning opportunities for their students, with greater opportunities for teachers to give their students individual attention. The Finnish approach to students with difficulties is early detection and intervention, rather than problem solving and individual support. With the assistance of a 'special teacher', students who need extra assistance are identified, and receive individual assistance based on learning plans developed for individual needs (OECD, 2010a). Every comprehensive school in Finland has a pupils' multi-professional care group, consisting of the principal, the special education teacher, the school nurse, the school psychologist, a social worker, the teachers whose students are being discussed and the parents where this is considered to be appropriate. The group meets at least every other week to discuss the classroom situation in general and particular students who face difficulties, and to decide on appropriate supports to be put in place. It is estimated that nearly two out of five students in Finnish schools have received part-time and full-time special interventions by the time they finish comprehensive school, which means that, in such an environment, special education is not considered 'special' (Pearson Foundation, 2011).

In Finland, teachers spend less time in lower secondary education compared to the average for OECD countries (OECD, 2010a). However, teachers commit much of their extra time to activities outside the classroom, including supporting students with special needs. More time is also invested in professional learning and applications to improve the school as a whole, and to improve classroom practice and work with the community (cf. Sahlberg, 2011b). Students with special needs are supported by a 'special needs teacher', working as a teaching assistant in the classroom. While the presence of a teaching assistant is beneficial, it may also create a potential barrier to participation. Excessive adult proximity allows children to overly depend on adults, or the particular teaching assistant, instead of seeking assistance from other children or the regular teacher. This can cause isolation and separation from other classmates (Takala, 2007: 51). An alternative approach comprises the provision of peer support by the teaching assistant instead of giving individual attention exclusively to the student. The assistant becomes an additional resource to support learning across the classroom rather than a *de facto* child-minder or individual tutor, as is the case in England (Farrell and Balshaw, 2002), the United States (Giangreco and Ruelle, 2008), and Australia (Bourke, 2009). Other concerns concerning teaching assistants in Finnish schools include the balance between their role of assisting teachers and children and poor work security, low salaries and limited opportunities for career progression (Takala, 2007).

Reform Initiatives in Inclusive Education

Research on reform initiatives in inclusive education reveals the inextricable link between historically ingrained social inequality and educational exclusion (cf. Ainscow et al., 2012). This is manifested in the quality and quantity of life opportunities in education, healthcare, housing, employment and various forms of social participation (Dyson et al., 2010). Canada, for example, ranks highly in literacy levels measured on test scores as well as in economic prosperity, but has been associated with poor performance in the areas of health and safety, family and peer relations, and subjective wellbeing (UNICEF, 2007). A mismatch between the levels of national wealth measured in GDP per capita and overall child wellbeing, including education and even material wellbeing, is also evident among some of the OECD nations – the USA, the UK, Austria and France are seen to rank lower in these regards compared to poorer nations such as the Czech Republic (Wilkinson and Pickett, 2009). In the state of California, Glass (2011) suggests that low educational achievement in schools is due to poor nutrition and health among disadvantaged children, which may have the effect of reducing concentration, school attendance and academic achievement. Slee (2010) argues that governments and researchers often portray the issue of poverty as 'pathological', rather than being socially constructed. It is treated as a political fact, rather than as 'an outcome of particular political, economic and social relations' (ibid.: 2). The implication of this is that the improvement of the quality of life for disadvantaged students can be enhanced by eschewing the reduction of education to human capital production through test score performance and by building social and community capital through focusing on local settings.

The success or otherwise of inclusive education practices hinges on the development of system-wide approaches to redefine desirable skills and qualities in education and being able to communicate these across diverse community contexts, while simultaneously building on individual school and community developments through networked local initiatives. Exclusive approaches and assumptions in policy reforms are considered to be barriers to the successful implementation of inclusion policies. For example, Dyson et al. (2010) suggest that the following approaches have resulted in ineffective policy reforms in the UK: policy being exclusively targeted at disadvantaged, low-attaining groups without taking into consideration the complex of inter-linked factors such as socio-economic arrangements in society and differences interpolated in language structures; prioritising structural reforms by adopting single issue responses rather than holistic interventions; a failure to 'resolve contradictions between state intervention and a reliance on centralisation on the one hand, and the promotion of an education marketplace with competitive and autonomous providers on the other' (ibid.: 5–6); and valuing a limited range of measured attainments over and against the full range of educational purposes.

Dyson et al. (2010: 27) suggest that politicians continue to propose 'solutions' under the assumption that the problem of inequality can be solved when they find 'a right combination of interventions and structural arrangements'. They warn us that this approach of targeting failing schools and underachieving groups will continue to fail so long as initiatives are 'overlaid on […] an inherently unfair system' and are 'compounded by the competitive, standards-driven nature of the system itself' (ibid.). Wilkinson and Pickett (2009), in their survey of affluent countries, surmise that, as a result, where inequality is high the country will rate at a lower level across a range of social indicators including education.

A Framework for Inclusive Education

To create a more equitable education system through reform, Dyson et al. (2010: 7) suggest three major and overlapping areas of concern: analysing local contexts; creating suitable learning opportunities; and establishing strong governance and accountability arrangements. In pursuit of this agenda, an emphasis on the local area is foregrounded. This helps stakeholders understand and respond to the presence of, and dynamic relationships between, social and cultural identities in the area, local needs, interests and resources, as well as the way education and relevant opportunities, public and private activities, are linked and coordinated. The analysis focuses on identifying these social, cultural, economic and political factors and complex ways in which educational inequalities are created so that the best strategies can be developed.

The second element, creating suitable learning opportunities, is a part of providing, 'learning opportunities for community engagement and development' (Dyson et al., 2010: 9). They suggest that in order to achieve greater equity across an education system, the curriculum, scope and opportunities for education need to reflect the characteristics of the locality, and stakeholders need access to diverse pathways that suit available employment and other future pathways and options for young people in the area. The identification and creation of such learning opportunities and future pathways requires the involvement of the whole community, including the family and local industry.

Governance and accountability arrangements address the issue of gathering data useful for teaching and learning (Black, 1998) that increases teachers' professional capacity and ownership of the process, in contrast to currently existing accountability regimes which have diverted practitioner's attention away from important elements of reform and teaching (Darling-Hammond and Rothman, 2011).

Finally, to enable such concerns to be implemented in order to accomplish inclusive education projects, the model suggests that high levels of professionalism and resilience need to be generated by the reform authority with all the stakeholders, including teachers, school staff and leaders, community workers, policy-makers and other relevant professionals (Hargreaves, 2009). In the previous chapter, we discussed the importance of vision and flexibility in the system to operationalise decentralisation (Levin, 2005). Flexibility within defined parameters is an important quality of school reform to allow for adjustments to the changing contexts of classrooms across complex central and regional educational jurisdictions (McLaughlin and Mitra, 2001). Figure 6.1 summarises these complex sub-elements in the proposed framework for inclusive education.

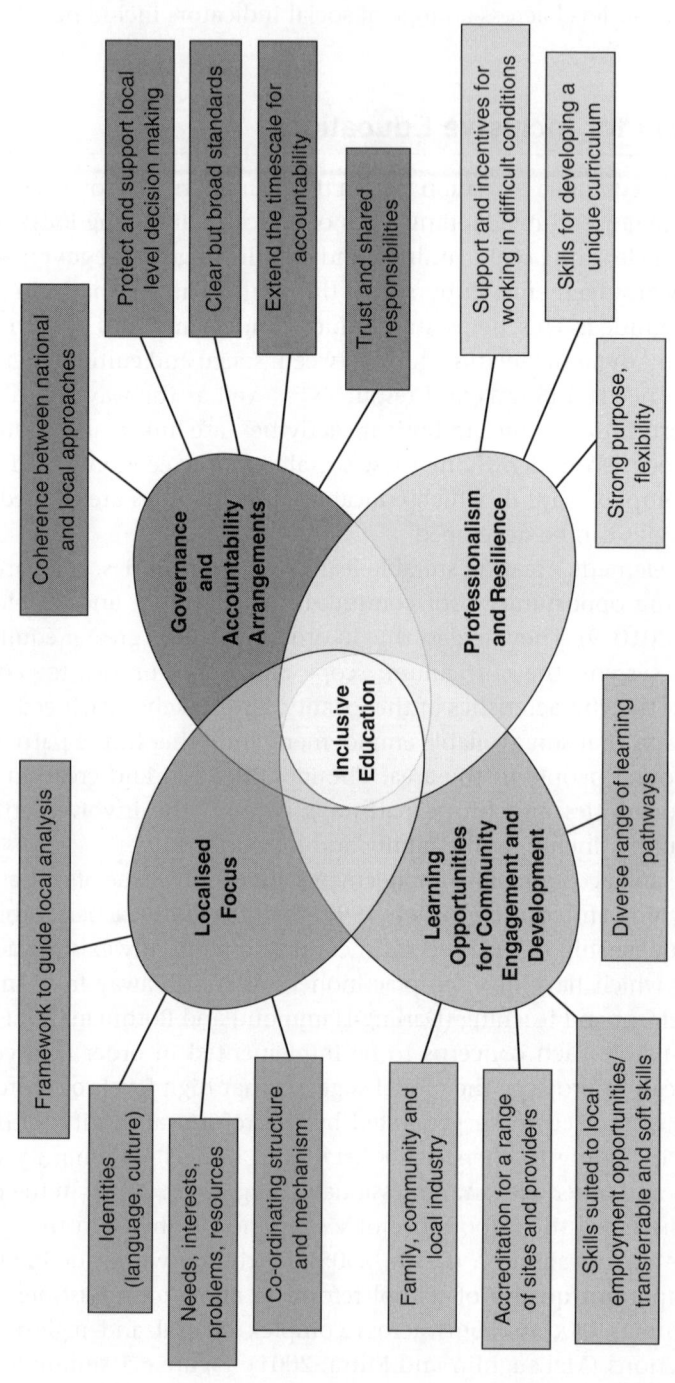

Figure 6.1 Framework for inclusive education

Figure 6.1 indicates the way in which the sub-elements are interconnected through the overlapping rings in the middle, which portrays a picture of the complex dynamics at play in systems reform. For example, curriculum development, reflecting local characteristics, needs and resources, requires advanced professional skills in teachers and education leaders, community connections and engagements, flexible accreditation systems, and a strong and supportive accountability system underpinned by coherent government policy frameworks. To enable students with diverse needs to learn in shared opportunities, teachers need to be resilient, supported by incentives and an understanding of needs guided by this framework.

Another example of a successful inclusion initiative is the most recent *Index for Inclusion* (Booth and Ainscow, 2011). This is an excellent resource for education systems seeking to reduce exclusion and build sustainable forms of inclusive schooling. Here, inclusive education is represented as an agent for providing fair and appropriate educational opportunities for disabled and disadvantaged children. The *Index for Inclusion* provides strategies for creating inclusive cultures, producing inclusive policies, and evolving inclusive practices in the school (cf. Ainscow, 2015). The focus is upon bringing the school community together to interrogate the nature and impacts of their school's culture, policies and practices. It has been translated into 40 languages and adapted for cultural specificities.

Global Citizenship, Global Education and Local/Personal Needs

While education for social inclusion involves the idea of localised identities and needs being reflected in its strategies, reform efforts also need to focus on the role of education in globalised societies, which potentially causes a dilemma. The relevant discussion of education for global citizenship takes the form of emphasising transportability and generic characteristics among educated people 'rather than those that solely entitle and enable participation in a relatively static local employment market' (Luke, 2004: 148). This phenomenon is apparent in, for example, the ongoing EU credentialing negotiations, which aims at loosening the boundaries through the professional degrees, credentials and registration, thereby making it a subject of free trade (Marginson and Considine, 2000). Luke (2004) argues, on the other hand, that the production of such job skills has reduced the aspect of moral and ethical training in the process of providing mass education.

Part of the strategy to challenge this tendency of mass education and lack of focus on individual capacity and needs was advanced through *personalised learning*, advocated across English and USA jurisdictions (Miliband, 2004). Personalised learning consists of teaching and assessment tailored to unique learning styles, motivations and needs of individual students. For example, assessment is used to feed into lesson planning and teaching strategies and goal setting by children. The high quality use of ICT provides flexibility to learning locations to engage in both individual and group learning. However, critics argue that this may merely be a move from, using synonyms of business terms, 'mass production to mass customisation' (Hargreaves, 2009: 2), without providing the necessary depth in learning, support, experience and leadership.

As a result, students 'access existing and unchanging kinds of conventional learning through different means ... [b]ut the nature of the learning itself is not transformed into something deeper, more challenging, and more connected to compelling issues in their world and their lives' (Hargreaves, 2009: 84). To achieve a high moral purpose in education, personalised learning can be conceived as a process of reconceptualising the fundamental nature of teaching and learning itself, and not just the mechanisms for delivering it.

In this model, an authentic process of personalised learning is an integral part of educating future citizens for global and knowledge economies, harnessing children's '[c]reativity, innovation, intellectual agility, teamwork, problem socialising, flexibility and adaptability to change' (ibid.). An important part of the process is to analyse the local context and develop pedagogical processes that are culturally responsive through problem-based learning while highlighting the way knowledge is built upon prior knowledge, i.e. children will connect what they have learned in the past with their engagement in the present. Below, we discuss contextual and cultural factors that affect equal access to education and, hence these are necessary considerations for establishing localised approaches for inclusive education.

Discussing local characteristics, needs and barriers potentially leads to distortions and contradictions across the system. Questions arise as to how much the education system needs to take into consideration, or make adjustments to account for, individual needs and diverse contextual and cultural differences. Here we defer to the suggestion that, through the outcome-focused accountability regimes we see in many education systems, inclusive education is increasingly concerned with the 'tolerance and management of presence and difference' (Allan, 2008: 15). Assessing the level of difficulty for a disabled child to access classrooms and participate in education, for example, is reduced to 'the nature and severity of their individual defects' (Slee, 2010: 123). As Slee maintains, disability and disablement need to be perceived as a social issue, which stems from a problem in the educational system itself. Therefore, the analyses of local characteristics need to investigate the dynamics of the way educational inequalities arise and 'relate to wider social and economic issues and how, in broad strategic term, the education system should respond' (Dyson et al., 2010: 9). Inclusion is not another term for special educational needs; it is a response to the difficulties of teaching across class, caste, religion, tribe, distance and gender inequalities.

System strategies are founded on the grounds that inclusion aims at 'removing social barriers that prevent equity, access and participation for all' and not about providing individuals with choices and changes (Rix, 2015: 276). For this, the principle of inclusive education needs to be represented and maintained by the community and organisational structures, so that coherent and systemic approaches to inclusive education can be established.

The system-wide and local analysis process is designed to identify not only particular barriers, but resources already available in the community. Here, it is the system that provides strategic leadership. Instead of focusing on where to ascribe blame and add regulations and sanctions to reduce blockages, these barriers are analysed so as to identify the complex relationship between education and disadvantage. This information is critical to enable the system to guide the formation of localised inter-agency partnerships in order to build robust inclusive education initiatives.

For example, in one local authority in England, it was assumed that the poor level of academic achievement among students was caused by students' low aspirations. However, it was quickly established that young people sought experience in the local job market instead of continuing their schooling. At the same time, they had a difficulty finding educational opportunities to improve their knowledge and job skills to advance their careers. In such cases, the local education authority might focus on providing flexible schooling and a curriculum that helps young people advance in the particular areas of skills that are useful for the local economy and beyond (Dyson et al., 2010: 8). Again, a localised analysis assists in reviewing existing school grants provision by the government to improve equal achievement levels among schools.

Inclusive policies can be encouraged through changing the financial arrangements in the system. In 1995, the New Zealand government introduced Targeted Funding for Educational Achievement (TFEA) as a component of the schools' operating grants. TFEA is targeted to assist schools to overcome barriers to students' achievement that are associated with socio-economic disadvantage. TFEA is not tied to any particular school activity. In 1998, the amount of grants provided to schools through TFEA was approximately $50 million; just over 7% of the $676 million was committed to overall operating grants in that year. Using the TFEA indicator, every state and state integrated school is ranked according to the presence of students from low socio-economic communities to determine funding allocations. Of all schools 10% are subdivided into 10 deciles and lower deciles comprise schools with more funding needs. Per-student funding is graduated; it increases as the school's decile declines. TFEA funding is allocated to decile 1–9 schools. According to the rate in 2010, per-student funding ranged from $NZ 819.75 for a decile 1A school to $26.18 for a decile 9 school (Ministry of Education, New Zealand, 2011).

Edge (2001: 8) explains that the TFEA socio-economic indicator is calculated using *census mesh-block* (a small geographic area) data together with schools' July ethnicity data. It takes into account household income, parents' occupation and educational qualifications, household crowding, parents' income support payments and Maori and Pacific Peoples' ethnicity. The rating is reviewed automatically every five years and can also be reviewed once per year if schools believe their SES make-up has changed significantly (e.g. because of a plant shutdown). Clearly, changes to the financial arrangements between central authorities and their schools have the potentiality to impact on the system in other ways and in particular on inclusive school initiatives.

Education for Migrant Children

The presence of immigrant, travelling and displaced children directly impacts upon the level of equal educational opportunities in many societies. Among OECD countries, net migration has tripled since 1960 and policy measures for accommodating migrants into local labour markets has become an important research focus, which includes the attempt to close academic achievement gaps between the native and migrant populations. According to the *OECD Reviews of Migrant Education* (OECD, 2010b), migrant children in general are characterised as having weaker educational outcomes at all levels compared to native students; they are less likely to attend early childhood education; they are more prone to drop out before the completion of upper secondary; they are more likely to attend schools with less favourable learning environments; and they have more language difficulties (OECD, 2010b).

Some of the factors that contribute to the poor performance of migrant, displaced and travelling children are: language problems, especially for those where the mother tongue, the language spoken at home, is different from the language of instruction at school; and their socio-economic background. The link between the language of instruction, especially at the primary school level, and school performance and equity has been well evidenced in comparative studies (Brook-Utne, 2007). In many developing countries, the fact that multilingualism is 'more the norm than the exception' makes it a critical issue (Mehrotra, 1998).

Another significant factor in the success or otherwise of migrant children in school is the high incidence of poor socio-economic backgrounds of their parents. The review conducted by the OECD (2010b) suggested three areas of economic vulnerability for immigrant parents: employment and earnings seem to fall significantly among immigrants; they are over-represented in unstable jobs, with less employment security and low skill levels; and, finally, they are more prone to become the subject of job discrimination. Parents' occupations and educational backgrounds impact on the availability of a favourable learning environment and assistance at home. This is an important factor, especially for children in early grades, and is generally associated with better academic performance. This applies to both native and immigrant students. These factors – language difficulty and the socio-economic background of parents – are found to be strongly associated with student performance, but there are also other unknown elements that account for poorer performance by immigrant students, since the study identified poorer performance among migrant children even after controlling for language and socio-economic effects (OECD, 2010a).

Other notable factors include lower participation rates in early childhood education nurseries and care institutions for immigrant children (OECD, 2010b). Participation in early childhood education and care institutions is found to have helped facilitate the integration of immigrant students. The review identified an increased chance of migrant children repeating or dropping out before completion of upper secondary and being over-represented in vocational or non-academic education programmes (OECD, 2010b). This tendency is more pronounced among first-generation immigrants than second-generation immigrants. Policy interventions for migrant children have similar effects to policy interventions for other types of disadvantaged children.

According to the review of existing strategies among OECD countries and other policy documents, it is possible to identify several contested strategies for inclusive education initiatives. These include: accommodation strategies versus integrative ones; a local openness to diversity versus particular supports for migrants; problem-based approaches versus population-based approaches; an emphasis on uniform achievement as against a fair balance of achievement between native and immigrant students; supply-side initiatives versus demand-side interventions; and a balance between rights and responsibilities.

The first of these is the tension between accommodation and integration. This raises the question of the effectiveness of using the mother tongue as the medium of instruction at the primary level (Mehrotra, 1998). Mother tongue instruction is 'a way to value assets which immigrant students already have' (OECD, 2010b: 16). For example, in Ireland, the national examination, which is a requirement at the end of compulsory education, is made available for some immigrants to allow them to use their native language. On the other hand, in some European countries from the 1990s onwards, such as The Netherlands, Austria, Denmark, Norway and Sweden, policy has shifted from accommodating cultural diversity towards greater integration. This policy shift, for instance in The Netherlands, imposes language proficiency as a condition for immigrants to enter the host society. Other countries increasingly emphasise 'strengthening host country language proficiency and sometimes explicitly de-emphasising mother-tongue instruction' (OECD, 2010b: 27). The policy setting requires coherence and coordination among different government departments, including education, immigration and employment. Education systems can act as a broker through the provision of policy leadership.

The second policy dilemma refers to the tension between local openness for diversity and support for migrants. Policy for migrant education has to confront the question of how strategy fits with wider educational goals. This created a problem since there may be a tension between favouring 'natives' greater openness to cultural and linguistic diversity and facilitating and supporting efforts to integrate immigrants' (OECD, 2010b). In most cases, however, the weight of policy is placed on the second area of concern and insufficient attention is paid to the concern for local openness for cultural diversity.

The third policy dilemma refers to the adoption of a problem-based approach as against a population-based approach. This tension is also described as 'universal' versus 'targeted' measures (OECD, 2010b: 15). It refers to whether policy measures will be established based on specific immigrant population target groups to close the gap between native and immigrant children, or general approaches to improve the system for both are adopted. The immigrant-targeted approach has been considered too narrow as it pathologises immigrant children and lowers teachers' expectations. The system challenge, we suggest, is in the efficient coalescence of both approaches because policy priorities may limit a targeted population, such as immigrant children, and hence do not allow holistic policy measures. Therefore, designing such measures may require careful policy negotiations.

The fourth tension concerns the balance between adopting a uniform approach as against a notion of fairness. When the achievement gap between population groups is too wide, it is possible that achieving the same academic levels among all students could be considered unrealistic, depending on the context. In such cases, policy-makers may need to set goals and strategies that focus on raising achievement among migrants, such as language proficiency, to a fair level compared to others.

The World Bank (2005) distinguishes two approaches in its policy discussion on increasing access to secondary schooling: 'supply-side initiatives' and 'demand-side interventions'. In many developing countries, the lack of access to secondary education is explained in part by affordability among the parents. In such situations, improving schools' conditions and teacher salaries in isolation, which is the 'supply-side initiative', is not the most effective policy focus. Instead, 'demand-side interventions' such as the conditional transfer of education, which allows flexibility of schooling in different locations, is suggested as the alternative approach (ibid.: 45). In the case of schooling of immigrant children, the OECD review (2010b) suggests that a poor educational environment is not caused by a lack of available educational resources in schools such as the number of teachers and physical facilities (OECD, 2006), but instead is due to environmental factors such as student absenteeism, a poor disciplinary climate and higher numbers of students pursuing vocational tracks.

Less-desirable learning environments at home also contribute to the situation. Education policy-makers need to consider both the supply-side and demand-side in their development of reform strategies to promote greater levels of educational inclusion and engagement for a range of diverse student populations. The approach favouring demand-side interventions comprises, for example, improving the environment at home through assisting migrant parents with language and skills to better assist children's learning at home and working with community groups and industry associated with these immigrant groups.

Finally there is the perceived tension between rights and responsibilities. Rights and responsibilities are complementary principles in education policy frameworks. Legislation and policy activity is needed to fuse these two important elements together. Sweden, for example, has a set of articulated 'social value and political commitments' that respect the languages, culture and heritage of immigrant students. They are committed to providing assistance for language support to immigrant students and adults. To make such political commitments effective, the OECD review emphasises the importance of communicating community rights and responsibilities, which clarify the expectations of government. For example, while the community respects their culture and heritage, immigrants are 'expected to bear the responsibilities of integrating in the host country, [such as by] learning the language of the host country, getting a job, paying taxes, respecting the given laws, sending children to school' (ibid.: 15).

The policy implications for including and engaging immigrant students that we have noted from the review (OECD, 2010b) suggest the need for a systems approach to inclusive education and policy reform that embraces coherence in priorities, messages and policy measures by relevant stakeholders, as it does for all the different types of disadvantaged students. Shared responsibilities, clear messages across stakeholder groups that include educators and the community, monitoring and research are essential to an inclusive education reform strategy.

> ... countries with relatively small performance gaps between immigrant students and their native peers have provided sustained and time-intensive language support in primary and secondary education [along] with clearly defined goals and standards for the teaching of the language of instruction. (OECD, 2010b: 46)

The OECD report also emphasises the importance of systematic support, which is integrated in curriculum structures and focuses on vulnerable conditions such as for older, first generation immigrant students (OECD, 2010b). Reflecting on our discussion of 'local analysis' earlier in this chapter, research can help policy-makers understand the current situation about migrant students from different perspectives and with their 'identification of different student groups can provide useful diagnostic evidence on which to base policy and design effective funding strategies' (OECD, 2010b: 17). This is the foundation that systems have pursued through evidence-based policy-making. It also allows policy-makers to identify available immigrant communities and parents as resources and pursue their involvement in first-language teaching and provide community role models. The OECD report suggests that the analysis of immigrant education should draw on research from many disciplines and methods, including research conducted as teacher practitioner action research.

As the Nobel Laureate from the University of Chicago, James Heckman argues, early childhood education is central to building inclusion, engagement and prosperity. Systems that establish inter-agency approaches to establishing early childhood interventions and education for immigrant, travelling and displaced populations limit the risk of failure in school. Concentration on children at their early developmental stages diminishes the reliance on welfare, health and justice systems for disengaged young people.

Building Schools as Communities

Over the last two centuries, industrialisation and the expansion of public education has opened access to education to wider sections of society including women, indigenous children and disabled children. However the transformation of schooling to mass education has forged education system hierarchies. Recent trends such as globalisation, standardisation and market-driven educational reforms have favoured high-stakes testing and accountability regimes that have contributed to a widening of the school-community gap. As Dyson et al. (2010: 5) report, 'education has been largely divorced from the communities where it takes place, the overriding emphasis being on individual and institutional attainment'. With broader societal challenges for schooling, the nature of teachers' work has become increasingly complex and demanding. With increasingly diversified societies and a new educational landscape, the involvement of both education and communities is an important factor in educational success (NIE, 2008). For this, teacher training and the structure of schools has to consider the contributions of new partners within the community. Through systemic reform, diverse institutions and stakeholders may be required to establish their complementary roles to make the reform initiative sustainable (Bishop et al., 2010). The community commitment to education also provides a rich ground for the successful implementation of decentralisation (cf. Lugaz and De Grauwe, 2010).

The growth of immigrant populations in the UK has increased the need for education that engages with and represents diversity. According to the census (Department for Education, 2010), almost 28% of pupils in state-funded primary and secondary schools in England (around 75% on average in Tower Hamlets) had a first language other than English. Their mother tongue represented about 240 different languages. Tower Hamlets in East London is one of the areas that comprise significant proportions of immigrant, traveller and displaced populations.

For example, Smithy Street Primary School is a state school where about 95% of its pupils come from the Indian sub-continent. Of these students 99% speak Sylheti, a dialect of Bengali/Bangla. The school has employed a bilingual educator to meet its unique language needs. Another 4% of children are Somali speakers and the rest, 1%, include Chinese and Urdu speakers. To celebrate this multicultural environment, the school holds after-school foreign language activities and multicultural events.

The provision of community languages support to the school by the Local Authority (LA) in Tower Hamlets is thought to be beneficial. Community languages are 'defined as all languages in use in a society, other than the dominant or national language' (McPake et al., 2006: 3). The provision of community languages (Uddin, 2009) started in the early 1970s in the community as after-school clubs with financial contributions from parents. It was believed that this provision supported improving children's learning and understanding of the curriculum, and intercultural understandings and competence in their English literacy skills as well as other languages. This provision has contributed to children's academic achievements, with improved outcomes in the General Certificate of Secondary Education (GCSE) examination in Bengali and Chinese, as well as reducing anti-social behaviour and small crimes by keeping children in a supportive learning environment after school. In 1995, the Local Authority established a centralised community language provision with public funding and extended its management to primary modern languages and the assessment of first languages among children.

Currently, the central team works with about 130 teaching staff who are recruited by the council's recruitment policy, work on contract, and are paid for by the Local Authority. The central team works with funded schools and community organisations including religious institutions and Idea Store, a community organisation that offers library services and other learning activities (Idea Store, 2011), and provides language and cultural learning activities for children aged 5 to 16. Many participating children are second and third generation immigrants. It has supported over 90 language projects in 13 different languages so far and about 5000 children attend its classes every evening (ibid.). The Local Authority's language provision also incorporates in their strategy pupils' language needs based on their visual, hearing and other sensory impairments and other communication related learning difficulties (Gatrell and Clifford, 2010). The provision is funded by a number of sources including community grants, charity organisations, trusts and parents. The funded schools and organisations it partners with are required to meet the quality assurance standards and to carry out self-assessments based on set targets, as the legislation holds the Local Authority accountable for ensuring that their relevant provisions meet the right quality of education as well as health and safety standards (Department for Education, 2010).

Among the 130 teaching staff, 22% have Qualified Teacher Status (QTS), 17% work at schools in various capacities, and 55% have teaching qualifications in language teaching obtained from a community college. The Local Authority offers in-service training to encourage tutors to develop their teaching careers (Uddin, 2009: 7). The Local Authority holds an Annual Language Celebration to involve students, tutors, parents and community leaders. It also works with a university to support research initiatives.

A review of the provision (Uddin, 2009) recommended enhanced collaborations between community language classes and the mainstream schools to foster learning relationships among them. Through this collaboration, teachers on both sides, as well as those who are directly involved, are able to continue to improve their pedagogies and their range of teaching activities, share ICT (information and communication technology) resources, encourage the use of the mother tongue in the family and community, and involve parents in discussions of their children's progress.

The effective engagement of the family and the community into school education requires a public awareness of the importance of education for social development, and trusting teachers as professionals and education leaders. Efforts were made to build awareness about the important contribution of education and those who are involved as well as some of the critical issues around education, in order to establish a supportive environment and promote active involvement of family and communities in their children's education. These are world-wide initiatives.

In Queensland, Australia, the State Education Week is an annual celebration to provide the community with 'the opportunity to recognise the talent and achievements of students and teachers in state schools, and showcase their wonderful work to the wider community' (Government of Queensland, 2011: 3). The initiative involves state-wide programmes, such as 'My Favourite Teacher', 'Principal for a Day', 'P&C [Parents and Citizens] Day' and 'Director General for a Day', as well as events hosted by individual schools to celebrate and profile their achievements. In Finland, the project Finland Needs Teachers was launched by the Trade Union of Education in 2002 to convey a more realistic and positive image of teaching to the general public, thereby raising awareness of teachers' work and its significant contribution to society (OECD, 2005).

In Ontario, Canada, each May, the province celebrates the Premier's Awards for Teaching Excellence to 'recognise educators and staff who excel at unlocking the potential of Ontario's young people' (Darling-Hammond, 2000: 6). In addition, in order to address the growing concerns about the negative effects of school ranking in the media, the province had established an agreement with the press not to mislead public opinion by converting complex school performance data into one-dimensional rankings (Fullan, 2007).

Inclusive Education Policies

In this chapter we have explored the implications of recent education policy developments for inclusive education. We have discussed current notions of diversity and exclusion in a globalising education context, and then proposed a framework for inclusive education. The focus here has been on productive practices relating to the removal of barriers to inclusive education. In some jurisdictions inclusive education merely describes education policies and practices for disabled (in both a physical and learning sense) students. We have taken a broader view of inclusive education as a response to all forms of educational exclusion. Inclusive education therefore refers to the dismantling of barriers to education for all students.

Inclusive education proceeds from an informed understanding of diversity and exclusion. Schools and school systems have always been powerful agents of exclusion. School organisation, the content of the curriculum and the values it expresses, the preferred form of teaching and learning, and assessment methods, combine to reinforce social elitism. This is true for many societies, developed or developing.

Many recent reforms to schooling have contributed to the exclusion of vulnerable children. Vulnerability may be associated with race, religious affiliation, poverty, disability, geographic isolation, gender or refugee status. Ranking schools on the basis of students' performance on tests encourages schools to be more selective. As we have suggested here, these practices have a deleterious effect upon minority groups and economically disadvantaged students. This is not a rejection of standards; rather it is a call for more inclusive pedagogical practices to support all students' access to participation and success in schooling.

The model of inclusion we favour in this chapter supports the view that increasing segregated special education provision for students with disabilities is not inclusive education. Committing scarce resources to a bifurcated system is wasteful. Lessons from jurisdictions such as Finland support the findings of Wilkinson and Pickett's (2009) study of inequality and social and economic wellbeing that aims to address inequality in schooling and other social institutions, and support the aspirations and strategies of inclusive education. Moreover, we suggest that a more inclusive approach to schooling can result in an overall improvement in achievement levels of students.

Developing more inclusive education that addresses the disadvantages experienced by children in scheduled tribes and castes, the girl child, disabled children and traveller and displaced children is achieved through teacher and community education as well as reforms to education policy. It is also important to attend to the curriculum as a key strategy to build more inclusive schooling. Evidence from the UK, Australia, Canada and New Zealand shows that when minority students are exposed to a curriculum that acknowledges their identity, they become more engaged with learning.

Inclusive education pivots on building schools as and with communities. Family community and schools share the aim of educating their children to enable them to optimise opportunities in life. Linking schools to their communities increases the number of teaching resources and leads to a broad engagement with and support for the education of all students. Education is therefore a civic enterprise; it is an apprenticeship in democracy (cf. Knight, 1985). As such, schools need to look at their own decision-making that represents the voices of stakeholders in these decision-making processes. Parent involvement in the school supports the achievements of the child. Schools need to be creative in designing platforms for parent participation. We now turn to the issue of inclusive practices in our recipient country, India.

Inclusive Practices in India

Issues of inequality have been present in India since the British Raj when the education system was exclusively focused on elites or the privileged. The country has improved its economic status recently and moved from low income to middle, or even high, income levels (though this is variable across social classes and castes), and it has shown a dramatic improvement in elementary enrolment in recent years, along with Ethiopia and Iran, which accounts for up to 93% (net enrolment) in 2011 (UIS, 2015). There are still nearly 290 million illiterate adults and about 1.4 million children out of school in India as of 2014 (UNESCO, 2014; UIS, 2015). The out-of-school ratio as a whole has declined by 73% since 1999 (UNESCO, 2014), with the number of out-of-school girl children reducing from about 10% in 2006 to 5% in 2014 (ASER, 2015). In Rajasthan, which is one of the poorest states, the rate dropped from about 20% to 11% during the same period.

Despite these promising trends, Shukla (1992) argues that the structure and content of education, which has an important bearing on reducing inequality, has remained essentially the same. In fact, the recent improvement in enrolment, which we noted above, may not reflect the actual situation, which is that in India as a whole there is still a high dropout rate from school. About 54% of elementary children leave school before grade seven and a large number of this group are girls (about 58%), the socially and economically disadvantaged, and first-generation learners. Although girls have an equal or higher primary enrolment rate than boys, the figure is less for secondary enrolment.

The issue of learning gaps is most obvious among older children. A study by UNESCO (2014: 33) suggests that nearly 90% of children aged eight or nearly eight answered a series of questions correctly in their grade-specific test, but only 33% of 14–15 year-olds did. In Vietnam, by contrast, the same age group (14–15 year-olds) achieved 71%. The UNESCO study drew the conclusion that the discrepancy between the two countries was due to the greater emphasis Vietnam placed on foundation skills in the primary curriculum and in particular to the attention it gave to disadvantaged learners. This suggests that there should be greater consideration given to these foundational skills, such as literacy and numeracy, by making the content and materials accessible to children with different language and cultural backgrounds. This includes a provision of on-going bilingual education and culturally relevant learning materials. However, this prioritises achievements in test situations, rather than following the curriculum per se.

The recent law, the Right to Education (RTE) Act, authorises schools to provide equal education opportunities for children with diverse backgrounds, including those from ethnic minorities. However, state, regional and local governments have found it difficult to recruit teachers from ethnic minorities who are prepared to teach children from ethnic minorities, and who are able to respond to children's language and cultural needs. The reason for this is that the education levels of ethnic minorities are often lower, and fewer enter teacher training institutes to become teachers. The states are rarely able to fill their caste-based quotas of teachers, and they often rely on teachers with lower levels of qualification (UNESCO, 2014).

Though the Indian government and state governments in their turn are committed to reducing gender inequalities in schools, putting in place structures to help girls succeed has had to overcome a series of political, socio-economic and cultural barriers, and is thus a slow incremental process. In India, reducing the gender literacy gap by 40% increased the number of women standing for state assembly elections by 16% and the share of votes that they received by 13% (UNESCO, 2014). Education has the potentiality to empower women and girls in their lives, and an example of this is that the freedom to choose your spouse is now becoming generally established. Women in India who graduated from secondary education were at least 30% more likely to have an influence over their choice of spouse than their less educated peers (UNESCO, 2014). Gender disparity in education is however affected by broader issues such as poverty, social values, inadequate school facilities, insufficient female teachers, and gender bias in the school curriculum. Traditional role divisions in households and society and stereotypes about gender are particularly strong in rural areas and disadvantaged communities.

In other words, improving women's lives and life chances through education is rarely sufficient. As a consequence, two different approaches to girls' education have been developed. The first of these, sometimes known as the Women in Development (WID) framework, entails incorporating women into development or education, and focuses on facilitating access and academic achievements through the supply of curricula, learning materials and so forth. The second approach, and in some ways oppositional approach, addresses issues to do with the transformation of women's lives through taking into account their living conditions and priorities, the gendered power balance in society, and community values that affect women's lives both for girls in school and also after formal schooling. Such interventions promote sex education, combat early marriage, ensure that women's rights are enshrined in law, attempt to change their relations with their parents, and develop community awareness. However, retention of girls in education cannot be achieved unless the two agendas and the practices emanating from them are coordinated. These interventions require commitments by state and local governments; however, officials in general neglect gender discriminations and such activity is mostly left to people working at the grassroots.

Issues of inclusive practices faced in India represent not only its complex systemic difficulties in education but also social and cultural dilemmas. The interventions comprise the allocation, and, in some cases, the reallocation of human resources and infrastructural values that are uniquely formed and coherent to the system. We have examined three different productive practices: teacher preparation and capacity, devolved governance and leadership to school levels and inclusive practices. In the last chapter we reflect on how the ideas associated with these three productive practices travelled to and impacted on the Indian education system.

7
POLICY LEARNING

Throughout this book we have been concerned with policy learning, and we understand this as identifying a set of practices which are considered to be successful in one national setting and then transferring them to another national setting, in which a problem or need has been identified. The policy that has been transferred is thought to be a solution to the problem or potentially able to meet this need, with the act of transfer understood as a learning activity. Previously, such models were thought of exclusively as processes of borrowing policy from other relevant countries or jurisdictions, and then turning these policies into practices, which were subsequently implemented.

The first of the models (P_1), referred to in Chapter 1, and developed by Philips and Schweisfurth (2008), focused on reconciling the external policy model, borrowed from countries or jurisdictions where it seemed to be operating in a successful or effective way, with local conditions in which these policies would be implemented. This consisted of providing a working model of the practice to be transferred, understanding how context impacted on that model – that is both contextual elements of the donor country or jurisdiction and contextual elements from the recipient country or jurisdiction – stripping out these contextual elements from the model being implemented and then replacing them with those contextual elements which were found to be of significance in the recipient country. As we noted, Philips and Schweisfurth understand this process as a series of steps, involving processes of conceptualisation (neutralising the questions to be addressed), contextualisation (providing a description of the issues against local backgrounds in two or more of the cases), isolation of differences (determining variances), explanation (developing an hypothesis), reconceptualisation (contextualising the findings) and application (generalising the findings). This model suffers from a common fault in knowledge transfer processes, which is that, it is assumed, context can be stripped out of these theoretical models without in some way distorting or impoverishing the models themselves, and that in like fashion recontextualising these models so that they are fit for the new environment does not in turn lead to a wholescale distortion of the original models. In short, it would be better to start from scratch and develop a model of a productive practice, which is wholly appropriate to the recipient setting. However, this would render the theory and process of policy transfer as fundamentally flawed.

There is a further problem with the model and this refers to the identification of good practice in the first place. There are a number of ways of identifying good practice. The first is identifying outputs from the system (these can be test scores, dispositional elements, acquired skills, ethical and moral qualities); that is, outputs that have resulted from the individual's participation in the mechanisms and workings of the system itself. The argument is then made that one system is better than another because it has better outputs, and, further to this, that the characteristics of these national systems should be bottled up and transferred wholescale to those countries or jurisdictions which are considered not to be successful or effective in these terms.

If the information collected about individuals in a system of education at the end of their time spent in the system is used to make judgements about the quality of provision within them, then there are two possibilities: using raw scores – student scores are aggregated to allow comparative judgements to be made about these schools, districts, states or nation states; and using value-added scores – value-added data analysis models the input of particular institutions or systems, such as schools, in relation to the development of individuals within these institutions or systems. There are three current meanings given to the term, value-added. The first of these is a measure of progress made by the individual where the prior attainment of that individual is taken into account. The second is a measure of progress where prior attainment as well as a range of other student and school factors outside the control of the school or nation is given due consideration. The third is a measure of progress where these background factors are controlled for but no control is exercised over prior attainment. Measurements such as these produce different results if different factors are taken into account. Most acceptable value-added analyses use a form of multi-level modelling, and this involves initial decisions being made about: background factors to be included in the modelling exercise; interaction factors for the model; the levels of hierarchy in the model; and the coefficients that it is assumed will be random at each level. Statistical relationships can as a result be calculated for relationships between different variables within the model.

As a result of these processes, a value can be attached to the input of the educational institution or nation as it has impacted on the progress of the individual(s) who attended it, or been a part of it. Indeed, because multi-level modelling is sophisticated enough to operate at different levels within the system, a value can be attached to the input of the unit being judged. Thus the modelling involved requires the researcher to make a number of decisions about which inputs to include and which relations to determine. The accuracy of such modelling depends on the belief that the educational researcher has in the reliability and validity of the data that is used, in the decisions they make about which variables to use in the modelling process, and also in the ability of the researcher to develop appropriate indicators or quasi-properties to reflect the actual properties of individuals, educational institutions and nations, and their covariance in real-life settings. Combining student scores (as outcome measures) and process observations in its turn requires the development of a methodology, or, to put it another way, a reliable and valid process to make comparative judgements between students, schools, districts, states or nation states.

A further way of determining quality in a system is by identifying a norm so as to allow a comparison to be made. For example, a system of education, whether international, national or local, can be compared with, and marked against, a model of best practice, where this model is constructed in terms of the inclusion of all the possible elements that could and should form an educational system (i.e. structures, institutions, curricula, pedagogic arrangements and evaluation protocols), their arrangement in the most logical way (for example, that curricular intentions should precede pedagogical approaches and indeed derive their credibility from these curricular intentions), and the identification and enactment of logically formed relational arrangements between these elements (i.e. that evaluation washback mechanisms should not be allowed to distort the curriculum as it was and subsequently has been conceived). The norm that is used comparatively in the policy transfer or indeed knowledge transfer process is constructed through sound logical and philosophical foundational principles. A reliance on outputs in the comparative process is unsafe and more importantly likely to be invalid.

Alternatives

We then suggested that the model proposed by Philips and Schweisfurth (P_1) could be usefully amended (to P_2). It still retains a notion of transfer and replacement of one context with another. And it still retains the element of transformation, prior to implementation. It is more precise about the activity sets at the different stages of the process. It now includes seven steps or phases. The first step is where the investigator conceptualises the focus of the investigation. She then identifies a mechanism within Country A (where this is the country from which the policy is being borrowed). A third step is understanding how this mechanism works in the context of Country A; in other words, identifying those factors within Country A which allow the mechanism to work as it was intended or at least as it has been adapted to a new set of circumstances (over time but still within Country A). A fourth step is identifying another country (B) which seems to be a suitable recipient of this mechanism, that is, it seems to have some similarities to the donor's context. A fifth step is identifying those similarities and differences between the contexts of the two countries. A sixth step is making a judgement about the degree of similarity and difference between the two settings and subsequently making a judgement about the amount and type of change required for the mechanism to work in Country B, which also requires a judgement to be made about whether the mechanism is working or not. This involves predicting how one mechanism which seems to work in one particular socio-historical setting should work in another which is characterised by a different set of structures. And finally, having identified the consequences of transferring the mechanism to the new country, the policy transfer is implemented.

A third model (P_3), and the one that we are advocating in this book, is a policy-learning model, and it therefore has built into it the characteristics of a learning process. An accepted, but not uncontested, view of learning is to theorise it as a process, with a range of characteristics. It has a set of pedagogic relations, that is, it incorporates a relationship between a learner and a catalyst, which could be a person, a text, an object in nature, a particular array of resources, an educational system or process, an artefact, an allocation of a role or function to a person, or a sensory object. A change process is required, either internal to the learner or external to the community of which this learner is a member. In any learning episode, there are temporal and spatial arrangements, and these can be understood in two ways: that learning is internally structured, and that learning episodes are externally located in time and space.

Further to this, learning is conditioned by an arrangement of resources. These arrangements are embodied, discursive, institutional, systemic or agential, and this has implications for the types of learning that can take place. Each learning episode has socio-historical roots. What is learnt in the first place is formed in society and outside the individual. It is shaped by the life that the person is leading. It is thus both externally and internally mediated, and the form taken is determined by whether the process is cognitive, affective, meta-cognitive, conative or expressive. Finally, learning has an internalisation element, where what is formally external to the learner is interiorised by this learner, and a performative element, where what is formally internal to the learner is exteriorised by them in the world. It is this performative element that is central to a policy-learning model; the learner (or learners) transfers their learning from one site to another, and in the process what is learnt is recontextualised within the new learning environment.

The first policy-borrowing model (P_1) focuses on the transformation of one set of descriptors about a policy mechanism into another so that the second set now fits the new circumstances in which the policy will be enacted. Here the contrastive assumption is that generalised knowledge can be produced through a process of identifying similarities and differences between a phenomenon and the circumstances in which it can be applied, and eliminating those factors which are not relevant to the transformative process. In the second policy borrowing model (P_2 adapted from P_1) there is a further assumption made that those descriptors refer to real events, happenings and mechanisms, and thus the transformational process has as its product a transformation of a material reality. The third and more significant model (P_3) builds an element of learning into the process and thus contextualises such learning both at the site of formation and at the site of implementation.

The Natural History of a Policy-borrowing Research Process

The research and development project that we refer to here, and have made frequent references to in this book is the International Best Practices Exchange leading to Innovation in Sarva Shiksha Abhiyan (SSA) project, coordinated by the national system of education in India and by Save the Children India, and funded by The European Union. The Institute of Education in the University of London was given an important role in the development of policy and practice within the overall project. We have made frequent references to it in the course of this book. This programme of research and knowledge transfer, as we have already indicated, employed a policy-borrowing model, and its recipient country was India. Current educational problems in India were identified as: poor teacher cadre management; limited models of inclusive education; and a weak capacity and disjointed systems for monitoring teacher performance and managing schools. The intention was to build the capacities of national and state level institutions and education departments in India by identifying, revising and implementing international models of best practice in the areas of teacher cadre management and performance, and school management and leadership, with a particular emphasis on inclusive education in a decentralised context. Further to this, the intention was to build the capacities of local education structures, through the development of inclusive learning environments based on a decentralised and participatory planning process.

At the outset of the project a series of meetings between Save the Children India, Save the Children UK and the Institute of Education research team to plan research and programme management took place. The next step comprised the identification of examples of international best practice in systems relating to teacher recruitment, management and performance, inclusive education practices, school management and decentralised planning, implementation, and monitoring systems. Consequently, the Institute of Education team produced a report that recommended a list of productive practices to be learnt from (cf. Terano et al., 2011). These included practices from the United Kingdom (teacher leadership and teacher cadre management; school-based management and inclusive education; curriculum development; schooling in multi-cultural neighbourhoods; and accountability frameworks through quality assurance mechanisms); Finland (school-based management; teacher development and management; and inclusive education); Australia (school-based management and teacher cadre management); New Zealand (processes of reform); Indonesia (school-based management) and Canada (curriculum and school-based management systems). The Thailand study was added through the efforts of Save the Children India as a separate study. Recommendations from the Thailand study focused on: school quality, teacher cadre management, and school-based management.

Following on from this, a national study in India of existing teacher cadre and management systems, issues and problems, with a specific focus on the seven pilot states where our work was to take place, was undertaken. The study objectives included: a mapping and synthesising of research on policies and implementation practices concerned with teacher recruitment, training (pre-service and in-service training) and management at the elementary stage within the national policy context; the identification, analysis and documentation of innovative and successful policy initiatives and good practices in teacher recruitment, management, training and teacher performance at the elementary stage at the state, district and sub-district levels; and finally, an analysis and documentation of the role played by decentralised governance in recruiting, managing and ensuring the performance of teachers.

And, in addition, a research study in India with particular reference to the selected states, to identify the current situation regarding thinking, policy and practice in inclusive education, school management, decentralised planning, implementation and monitoring systems, was undertaken. The objectives of this study were to: analyse and document existing good practices in school management, including leadership and inclusive teaching and learning processes to combat exclusion in schools; map and synthesise research on policies concerned with school management with particular reference to good quality inclusive education and decentralisation; and analyse and document innovative good practices that provide support to decentralised planning and governance in facilitating inclusive education of disadvantaged groups of children, as well as good practices in providing good quality inclusive education that can be achieved through processes of decentralisation.

The research report reviewed the education policies of eight states. The report was published in 2013 by the National University of Educational Planning and Administration (NUEPA). A synopsis of the study was also published alongside the main report to capture its key points for the benefit of policy-makers and senior government officials. In conjunction with this, a needs assessment was conducted in five states (Andhra Pradesh, Delhi, Jammu and Kashmir, Rajasthan and Odisha). Gujarat and Himachal Pradesh were added in year two of the project for the baseline assessment. The objectives of the survey were to collect baseline data to measure the impact of the intervention under identified indicators, and, based on the baseline study findings, to produce recommendations for the effective implementation of the project.

In order to disseminate the work of the project in its initial stages, both the international and national studies were published and shared with all the state SSA departments and major educational institutions in the country. The technical advisors of the respective states developed presentations on the key findings of the studies and shared them during various state meetings, workshops and forums. The key recommendations arising from the studies were disseminated at state, district and cluster levels in the respective forums as well.

A national steering committee (NSC) was formed at national level and consisted of representatives from the National University of Educational Planning and Administration, the National Council of Educational Research and Training, education officials from the intervention states and Save the Children India. (The Institute of Education was deliberately excluded.) The National Steering Committee was encouraged to function as a critical forum to bring together education stakeholders to facilitate the sharing of learning experiences at national and international level and help achieve an effective and coordinated programme across departments. The National Steering Committee was also envisaged as a national level forum where stakeholders would collaboratively explore the possibility of reform in the areas of teacher cadre management, teacher education, performance assessment systems and school management systems with the focus on decentralisation and inclusive education. In addition, a state level core group in each project state composed of district and state level decision- and policy-makers, was set up to review best practice, elect representatives to participate in international best practice exposure visits and exchanges, and arrange quarterly progress reviews and implementation planning meetings.

Five district level sub-committees were subsequently convened in selected districts of Delhi, Jammu and Kashmir, Andhra Pradesh, Odisha and Rajasthan, comprised of district level decision-makers, cluster resource representatives, local governance personnel, children and school management officials, to meet monthly to monitor the implementation of international best practice models at district level and to facilitate the exchange of information between state and cluster levels. They were also designed to facilitate stakeholder forums and meetings for teachers and cluster representatives at cluster levels to assess current implementation problems and identify opportunities for utilising models of international best practice to address and improve these practices. Their aim was to coordinate stakeholder forums and meetings at village level, including Village Education Committees, School Management Committees, Children's Groups, and Parent Teacher Associations.

A large cohort of master trainers was trained at the state level in systems analysis, child rights and participation, and the introduction of best practice in education. These master trainers were tasked with the training of a large number of teachers/ supervisors on training and facilitation skills, problem identification, system analysis, inclusive education, child rights and participation, the sharing of best practices at state level, as well as specific training based on initial needs assessment.

The next stage was the convening of an international conference involving key stakeholders such as State Education Secretaries, Commissioners of Public Instruction, State Project Directors of SSA and Directors of Elementary Education in India, and key policy-makers and practitioners from the European Union and elsewhere, to facilitate the exchange of information on international best practice models of teacher cadre and school management.

An international field study tour was organised by Save the Children with officials from Sarva Shiksha Abhiyan (SSA), the National University of Educational Planning and Administration and the Ministry of Human Resource Development to the United Kingdom and Finland in 2011. A total of fifteen members visited the two countries. The purpose of the visit was to study the innovations and best practices in the areas of teacher cadre management, school-based management and inclusive practices with reference to India. The second study visit was organised to Thailand and Australia. Seventeen officials from the MHRD, NUEPA, Andhra Pradesh, Gujarat, Odisha, Rajasthan, Karnataka, Haryana, Madhya Pradesh and Assam took part. Delegates from Karnataka, Haryana, Madhya Pradesh and Assam were part of the delegation as these states were added by MHRD for the purposes of the study visits.

Selected participants from the core group in the seven states attended needs-based training placements in Europe and elsewhere internationally. National level workshops were arranged to explore international practices in educational systems with key stakeholders, policy-makers and practitioners from India, the EU and elsewhere. This allowed the development of school development plans in consultation with children, parents, teachers, PTA and VEC representatives to bring best practice models of teacher development, devolved governance and inclusive education to the school level, and the development of programme implementation plans at cluster and district levels. Finally, the research and policy-borrowing process concluded with an international conference in Delhi to present its findings and develop ways of taking the reform process forward. In the end, the authorities at the central level were more interested in the possibility of developing a national inspection service, along the lines of the United Kingdom's OFSTED Inspection service, rather than any of the other initiatives being offered. In respect of this they were given highly partisan and one-sided presentations about OFSTED's work and how it could transform the Indian educational system, for example, the OFSTED process was described as formative and non-punitive.

The Failure of the Reforms

There are three pitfalls with the policy-borrowing model that we have referred to throughout the book. The first is that the mechanisms, structures, instruments and apparatus, in short, the productive practices, can be misrepresented or at the very least only partially represented, so that particular and ideologically framed versions are received. This is because carefully constructed views of the countries from the field study tours were framed and packaged for the participants. The learning environments or spatio-temporal settings for learning that the study tours were set up to provide consisted of typically short presentations by the relevant authorities and carefully guided observations of what they considered to be important instances of their practices. No thought was given to the learning process on these study tours.

Second, there is an issue as to the actual degree of power and influence held by participants on these study tours. Did they have the power to make a difference? As we suggested in Chapter 4, a distinction can be drawn between attributability and responsibility as accountability (Aristotle, 1925), and this distinction rests on the difference between ascribing moral responsibility to a person or organisation because they or the organisation is formally responsible for their or its activities and only making someone or some organisation responsible if they were in a position to do something about it and thus effectively make a difference. This last involves a judgement about what is reasonable in attributing responsibility to a person or organisation in the actual circumstances in which those activities were performed and about which that judgement is being made.

Third, the structure of the study tours, i.e. their content, their observational focus, their timings and the pedagogical instruments they used, was decided at central government level. This included which countries were considered to be appropriate, the topics that were to be discussed, the areas that were to be observed, the methods that were to be used and even the conclusions participants were expected to come to.

The issue then is whether these were appropriate conditions for learning to take place. We have already suggested that these learning environments were carefully chosen and constructed by important Indian government officials working in conjunction with the NGO; that no thought was given to the learning process during these study tours; and that no attempt was made by participants to genuinely understand how the various practices and mechanisms actually worked in the conditions in which they were being observed.

A set of ideas about learning, and subsequently a learning practice, pivots on the idea that there is an entity called for the sake of convenience a human and that this entity has a relationship (both inward and outward) with an environment. A learning approach specifies the circumstances in which it can be used in the learning environment; the resources and technologies which allow that learning to take place; the type of relationship between teacher and learner, and learner and learner, to effect that learning; a theory of learning, or, in other words, a theory of how that construct (i.e. knowledge set, skill or disposition) can be assimilated; and a theory of transfer held by the teacher, that is, how the learning which has taken place in a particular set of circumstances (i.e. a classroom, with a set of learners, in a particular way, with a particular theory of learning underpinning it, and so forth) can transfer to other environments in other places and times. These elements were clearly missing from the actual environments that our study tourists were placed within.

It might be appropriate to think about this problem in a different way, and to reconceptualise it as an example of surface rather than deep learning. Learners who take a deep approach have the intention of understanding, engaging with, operating in and valuing the object that is to be learnt. Such learners actively seek to understand this object; interact vigorously with the content; make use of evidence, inquiry and evaluation; take a broad view and relate ideas to one another; are motivated by interest; relate new ideas to previous knowledge; and relate concepts to everyday experience.

Learners who take a surface approach tend not to have the primary intention of becoming interested in and of understanding the subject, but rather their motivation tends to be that of fulfilling the requirements of the activity and passing on this learning to a higher authority, where actual decisions are made about policy and practice. Learners who take a surface approach try to learn in order to repeat what they have learned; memorise information needed for the minimal requirements of the job; make use of rote learning; take a narrow view and concentrate on detail; fail to distinguish principles from examples; and are motivated by fear of failure. Marton and Säljö (1976) termed this the 'surface approach'. On the contrary, learners could have treated the text – the set of practices and ideas with which they were confronted – as containing a structure of meaning. If they had done this, they would have searched for its underlying concerns, its implications and its meaning for themselves. Marton and Säljö (1976) termed this the 'deep approach'.

In the end, very little was achieved. The key achievements of the project were described by Save the Children in the final report as:

- The completion of a baseline survey, management information system reviews of all the seven project states and its presentation in the respective state core group meetings.
- The completion of an international study focusing on international productive practices in education and two national level research studies focusing on teacher recruitment, training, management and performance; school management for quality inclusive education and decentralised school governance to identify best practices in teacher recruitment, management and performance; school management and inclusive education. The national studies were published in collaboration with NUEPA.

- Rapport building and greater engagement with key government officials and duty bearers at the national, state, district and school level.
- The formation of a National Steering Committee at the national level along with the state core groups at the state level that gave the impetus to the project with the district level committees in supporting the micro level activities.
- The Establishment of eight National Steering Committees during the project's time span.
- The completion of two international study visits for 30 national and state officials to the UK, Finland, Thailand and Australia in order to gain an understanding of the productive practices from these countries.
- The completion of technical placements for 45 education personnel from State and National education departments and Institutes in the area of School Leadership, Teaching and Learning Standards and Inclusion in the UK.
- The setting up of an international conference on 'Transforming Schools for Quality Education'. Government officials from 15 states of India and academics/policy-makers from six different countries attended the conference.
- Delivering four thematic workshops on Curriculum Development, Inclusion in Education, School Leadership and Teaching and Learning Standards, attended by 130 education officials from the project states.
- Findings from these international visits were utilised to draft and finalise state reform proposals, and the inclusion of the reform areas in the Annual Work Plan of SSA of Andhra Pradesh, Odisha, Himachal Pradesh, Gujarat, and Rajasthan.
- The completion of a mid-term review report, an end-line report and an end-term evaluation report of the project.
- The establishment and capacity building of Children's Groups in project schools of Delhi, Andhra Pradesh, Jammu and Kashmir, Rajasthan and Odisha. Children's Groups have been formed in 400 schools in the project areas.
- The employment of 280 state master trainers in seven states to train teachers.
- The training of 1186 teachers from 450 schools in five project states to facilitate and develop schools as inclusive learning environments.
- The translation of International and National Studies in Ladakhi, Hindi, Gujarati, Telegu and Oriya.
- The completion of national workshops on School Leadership, Teaching and Learning Standards and Inclusion in Education.
- The completion of a National Dissemination workshop and conference in which 150 senior government officials from 32 states participated. Final State Reform proposals were presented during the workshop and work completed under the project was highlighted.

It should be noted here that most of these achievements relate to the setting up of systems and few to actual solid achievements at the classroom level, and certainly, though the project did make some changes to the education system as a whole, it is doubtful whether the successful elements of the change process actually originated from the study tours and thus from the international comparative policy borrowing elements of the project.

Policy-learning Environments

We have referred here to productive practices, reflecting our concern that the focus needs to be on how practitioners learnt from the work and experience of each other, rather than on the apparently exemplary practice itself. Equally, we did not see learning from international comparative experience as a passive process of policy borrowing. Because we saw the jurisdictions and countries that emerged from the themed productive practices as productive locations for learning, the effectiveness of this type of project to some extent depended not on the practices adopted in the countries studied, but on the quality of the learning derived from them. The focus then was on generative practices rather than on generalising educational practices across very different contexts.

Learning comprises a change to the status quo, to what already exists. What this means is that the same learning object is likely to have different effects on different learners and on different occasions on the same learner. Knowledge then is transformed at the recipient site, and this includes for our purposes here those arrangements in the system where learning and change can take place. Most education systems are resistant to change and provide few opportunities for both learning and transformation, and India is a good example of this. For example, a key principle of the administrative structure for education in this country is that at national and state levels, administrators and policy-makers, many of them specialising in areas other than education, were frequently moved from one position to another. This loss of organisational knowledge at key points in the process meant that reforms as they are envisaged rarely achieve their potential and the International Best Practices Exchange leading to Innovation in Sarva Shiksha Abhiyan (SSA) project was no exception.

In constructing a theory of learning, there is a need to understand the constitution of the learning object (i.e. its structure and grammar), which is then animated by the learning process. A learning object's effect and history can be categorised in four ways: the capacity of the object to change the present state of affairs, the sustainability of the integrity of the object during the process, the malleability of the receiving schema (cf. Piaget, 1962), and the transformative potential of the learning experience. All of this amounts to a set of relations between a cognising subject and the social and natural worlds.

The first of these is the capacity of the learning object to change the status quo. This refers to the structure of the learning object or the way it is constituted. Some of these learning objects are crafted so that, even given the state of the schema into which they are being introduced, they have a more fundamental impact than other forms of learning. The second is the sustainability of the integrity of the object over time. What we are referring to here is the capacity of the learning object to retain its original shape, form and content in the learning process. When we refer to the integrity of a learning object, we do not understand this in an ideal sense. A learning object is always an amalgam of different ideas, values and prescriptions, which is never completely coherent. What this suggests, however, is that in the long process of formulation, to internalisation, through to realisation, and thence to performance, the original integrity of the learning object is either strongly or weakly maintained.

The third feature is the malleability of the receiving schema, and this in turn points to the degree of resilience of the schema, or the capacity to resist or allow learning to take place. Learning has a greater or lesser capacity to impact on and change these schemas, and in part this refers to how it is going to be introduced, but also to the constitution of the learning object. Its penetrative power (though this may not be realised) or capacity to effect change is different in different learning episodes. This is the intensity of the learning object, and clearly its obverse is the resilience or otherwise of the current arrangements within the individual's mind. This is the malleability of these arrangements. Then there are the performative elements of the learning experience, and these refer to the capacity of the learning process to feedback into the environment, both the natural and social worlds and the learning process itself.

These learning models are characterised by a relation between an internal and an external process, and learning is social, both in the sense that learning takes place in society and with people in society, but more fundamentally, because the contents and processes of learning are social phenomena. We are therefore confronted in relation to learning with a particular set of relations between external structures and internal or agential processes, and it is the particular relations between the two that produces learning.

In any learning sequence, the learner is confronted with a set of ideational resources or structured discourses, and in addition, she is embedded in another set of structures, which refer exclusively to her sense of agency. These structures of agency mediate, for the individual learner, entry into those discursive structures which act as a resource for her belief system; as a result, learning theorists are required to confront notions of formal and informal learning and therefore of assimilation, discarding, layering, organising, synthesising, selecting, and meta-processes connected to learning. Discursive structures may be characterised as those ideational resources which sustain the learner, and they include a range of stories, narratives, arguments and chronologies that have a number of distinctive features: they have a specific time–place location, and thus are subject to change and amendment; they are structured in turn and thus different patterns of story-telling or narrative genre are possible; and they compete with other genres. In addition, they play a role in the construction and maintenance of structures of agency.

It is this relationship then between these structures and the agential capacity of the learner which determines whether and in what way learning can take place. These relational modes have five forms. The first refers to the knowledge-ability of the learner, that is, the amount and type of knowledge held, with this type of knowledge comprising cognitions, skills and dispositions. The second relational mode again refers to the agential learner but this time to those factors which impact on the knowledgeability of the agent, i.e. unconscious beliefs, unacknowledged conditions of action, tacit knowledge and unintended consequences. The third relational mode refers to the degree and type of give in the structure, and each type has a different shaping capacity. An embodied structure such as a notion of sexuality, compared with a discursive structure is an example of this, and this is in part because the discursive structure can in certain circumstances be ignored, though there are consequences or sanctions as a result. The fourth relational mode refers to the degree and type of give in the agent or in those structures of agency, which provide the conditions for those agents to make the decisions they do. And finally, the fifth mode refers to the consequences of that relation in learning. There are different consequences depending on the type of relation that is implicated in the learning episode. Any model of policy borrowing then above all else has to be a learning model. Learning is not then treated as a decontextualised activity, but as the essential building block of transformative approaches to policy and practice in and between nations.

Education policies are increasingly being enacted on a global stage. Comparisons of system performance and of the performance of different parts of school systems play a critical role in national policy-making. Policy exchange – policy borrowing or, perhaps, policy theft – is a feature of education reform globally. We suggest that the emphasis placed on policy exchange is unlikely to diminish; indeed, our experience in developing this book is that there is an added urgency to the process as governments examine with even greater impatience the performance of their school systems. We have argued in this book that the policy-borrowing model, as it is currently conceived through a lens of edu-tourism and policy translation, is conceptually flawed as a solution to improving education systems round the world. However, we are not naïve about the need to improve school systems, and for productive practices of improvement to be exchanged. Our view is that there is much to be gained by reframing the current policy exchange model, so that the focus of international attention is now on policy learning and the creation of productive learning environments round the world.

REFERENCES

Ainscow, M. (2015) *Struggles for Equity in Education*. Abingdon: Routledge.
Ainscow, M., Dyson, A., Goldrick, S. and West, M. (2012) *Developing Equitable Education Systems*. Abingdon: Routledge.
Alexander, W. (1954) *Education in England: The National System, How it Works*. London: Newnes.
Allan, J. (2008) *Rethinking Inclusive Education: The Philosophers of Difference in Practice*. Dordrecht: Springer.
Annual Status of Education Report (ASER) (2015) *ASER 2014: Annual Status of Education Report*. Delhi: Pratham.
Aristotle (1925) *Nicomachaen Ethics (Ethica Nicomachea)*, trans. W.D. Ross. Oxford: Oxford University Press.
Aspin, D. (1996) 'The liberal paradox', in J. Chapman, W. Boyd, R. Lander and D. Reynolds (eds), *The Reconstruction of Education: Quality, Equality and Control*. London: Cassell.
Aubrey, B. and Cohen, P. (1995) *Working Wisdom: Timeless Skills and Vanguard Strategies for Learning Organizations*. San Francisco: Jossey Bass.
Ball, S. (1990) *Politics and Policy Making in Education: Explorations in Policy Sociology*. London: Routledge.
Ball, S. (1994) *Education Reform: A Critical and Post-structural Approach*. Buckingham: Open University Press.
Ball, S. (2007) *Education plc: Understanding Private Sector Participation in Public Sector Education*. London: Routledge.
Ball, S. (2008) *The Education Debate*. Bristol: Policy Press.
Bandura, A. (1977) *Social Learning Theory*. New York: General Learning Press.
Barber, M. with Moffit, A. and Kihn, P. (2011) *Deliverology 101: A Field Guide for Education Leaders*. Thousand Oaks, CA: Corwin.
Barnes, C. and Mercer, G. (2005) *The Social Model of Disability: Europe and the Majority World*. Leeds: The Online Disability Press.
Barton, L. (2005) *Special Educational Needs: An Alternative Look. A Response to Warnock*. Available at: www.leeds.ac.uk/disability-studies/archiveuk/barton/Warnock.pdf.
Bauman, Z. (2004) *Wasted Lives: Modernity and its Outcasts*. Oxford: Polity.
Bhaskar, R. and Danermark, B. (2006) 'Meta-theory, interdisciplinarity and disability research: A critical realist perspective', *Scandinavian Journal of Disability Research*, 8(4): 278–97.
Bishop, R., O'Sullivan, D. and Berryman, M. (2010) *Scaling up Education Reform: Addressing the Politics of Disparity*. Wellington: NZCER Press.
Black, P.J. (1998) *Testing: Friend or Foe?: Theory and Practice of Assessment and Testing*. London: Falmer.
Black, P.J. and Wiliam, D. (2009) 'Developing the theory of formative assessment', *Education Assessment, Evaluation and Access*, 21: 5–31.
Black-Hawkins, K., Florian, L. and Rouse, M. (2007) *Achievement and Inclusion in Schools*. Abingdon: Routledge.

Booth, T. and Ainscow, M. (2011) *The Index for Inclusion*. Bristol: Centre for Studies in Inclusive Education.

Borko, H. (2004) 'Professional development and teacher learning: Mapping the terrain', *Educational Researcher*, 33(8): 32.

Bourdieu, P. and Passeron, J-C. (1977) *Reproduction in Education, Society and Culture*. London: Sage Publications.

Bourke, P.E. (2009) 'Professional development and teacher aides in inclusive education contexts: Where to from here?', *International Journal of Inclusive Education*, 13: 817–27.

Bowles, S. and Gintis, H. (1976) *Schooling in Capitalist America: Educational Reform and Contradictions of Economic Life*. New York: Basic Books.

Boyd, W. and Chapman, J. (1987) 'State-wide educational reform and administrative reorganisation: Australian experience in American perspective', in W. Boyd and D. Smart (eds), *Educational Policy in Australia and America: Comparative Perspectives*. Lewes: The Falmer Press.

Brantlinger, E. (2006) *Who Benefits from Special Education? Remediating (Fixing) Other People's Children*. New Jersey: Lawrence Erlbaum Associates.

Brook-Utne, B. (2007) 'Learning through a familiar language versus learning through a foreign language – a look into some secondary school classrooms in Tanzania', *International Journal of Educational Development*, 27(5): 487–98.

Brundrett, M., Fitzgerald, T. and Sommefeldt, T. (2006) 'The creation of national programmes of school leadership development in England and New Zealand: A comparative study', *International Studies in Educational Administration*, 34(1): 89–105.

Bruner, J. (1996) *The Culture of Education*. Cambridge, MA: Harvard University.

Caldwell, B. (2000) 'Leadership in the creation of world class schools', in K. Riley and K. Louis (eds), *Leadership for Change and School Reform*. London: Routledge Falmer.

Caldwell, B. (2008) 'Reconceptualising the self-managing school', *Educational Management, Administration and Leadership*, 36(2): 235–52.

Caldwell, B. and Hayward, D. (1998) *The Future of Schools: Lessons from the Reform of Public Education*. London: Falmer.

Cardno, C. and Youngs, H. (2013) 'Leadership development for experienced New Zealand Principals: Perceptions of effectiveness', *Educational Management Administration and Leadership*, 41(3): 256–71.

Chapman, J. and Aspin, D. (1997) 'Autonomy and mutuality: Quality education and self-managing schools', in T. Townsend (ed.), *Restructuring and Quality: Issues for Tomorrow's Schools*. London: Routledge.

Chapman, J., Dunsan, J. and Spicer, B. (1996) 'System restructuring: School based management and the achievement of effectiveness in Australian education', in J. Chapman, W. Boyd, R. Lander and D. Reynolds (eds), *The Reconstruction of Education: Quality, Equality and Control*. London: Cassell.

Corbett, J. and Slee, R. (2000) 'An international conversation of inclusive education', in F. Armstrong, L. Barton and D. Armstrong (eds), *Inclusive Education: Policy, Contexts and Comparative Perspectives*. London, UK: David Fulton. pp. 133–46.

Czarniawska, B. and Sevon, G. (2005) *Global Ideas: How Ideas, Objects and Practices Travel in the Global Economy*. Malmo: Liber and Copenhagen Business School Press.

Darling-Hammond, L. (2000) *Powerful Learning: What We Know about Teaching for Understanding* (1st edn). San Francisco, CA: Jossey-Bass.

Darling-Hammond, L. and Rothman, R. (2011) 'Lessons learned from Finland, Ontario and Singapore', in L. Darling-Hammond and R. Rothman (eds), *Teacher and Leader Effectiveness in High-Performing Education Systems*. Washington, DC:

Alliance for Excellent Education/CA: Stanford Center for Opportunity Policy in Education. pp.1–11.
Department for Education (2010) *Schools, Pupils and their Characteristics*. Available at: http://www.education.gov.uk/rsgateway/DB/SFR/s000925/index.shtml (accessed on 20 April 2011).
Dorling, D. (2010) *Injustice: Why Social Inequality Persists*. Bristol: The Policy Press.
Dyson, A., Goldrick, S., Jones, L. and Kerr, K. (2010) *Equity in Education: Creating a Fairer Education System: A Manifesto for the Reform of Education in England*. University of Manchester: Centre for Equity in Education.
Easton, D. (1979) *A Framework for Political Analysis*. Chicago: University of Chicago Press.
Edge, K. (2001) *School-Based Management: Q&A for the Web/Knowledge Nugget*. Washington, DC: World Bank.
Engeström, Y. (2001) 'Expansive learning at work: Toward an activity theoretical reconceptualization', *Journal of Education and Work*, 14(1): 133–56.
Eskay, M., Onu, V., Igbo, J., Obiyo, N. and Ugwuanyi, L. (2012) 'Disability within the African culture', online submission, *US-China Education Review*, 4: 473–84.
Etzioni, A. (1961) *A Comparative Analysis of Complex Organisations*. New York: Free Press of Glencoe.
Farrell, P. and Balshaw, M. (2002) *Teaching Assistants: Practical Strategies for Effective Classroom Support*. Beverly, MA: Fulton.
Foucault, M. (1979) *Discipline and Punish: The Birth of the Prison*. New York: Vintage.
Fullan, M. (2007) *Leading in a Culture of Change*. New York: Jossey Bass.
Fullan, M. (2014) *There is Something Different about 2014*. New York: Jossey Bass.
Gagné, R. (1985) *The Conditions of Learning*. New York: Holt, Rinehart and Winston.
Gatrell, L. and Clifford, N. (2010) *Carers Joint Strategic Needs Assessment*. London: Tower Hamlets and the National Health Service.
Giangreco, M. and Ruelle, K. (2008) *Teaching Old Logs New Tricks: More Absurdities and Realities in Education*. New York: Peytral Publications.
Gillborn, D. and Youdell, D. (2000) *Rationing Education: Policy, Practice, Reform, and Equity*. Buckingham: Open University Press.
Glass, R. (2011) 'Re-imaging "public education"'. Keynote address at The Doctorate? BELMAS Doctoral Research Interest Group Seminar Series (28 March), Institute of Education, University of London.
Glatter, R. (2012) 'Persistent preoccupations: The rise and rise of school autonomy and accountability in England', *Educational Management Administration and Leadership*, 40(5): 559–75.
Gough, N. (1999) 'Surpassing our own histories: Autobiographical methods for environmental education research', *Environmental Education Research*, 5(4): 407–18.
Government of Queensland (2011) *State Education Week*. Available at: http://education.qld.gov.au/projects/educationviews/news-views/2011/mar/state-education-week-110316.html (accessed 28 April 2011).
Graham, L. and Slee, R. (2008) 'An illusory interiority: Interrogating the discourse/s of inclusion', *Educational Philosophy and Theory*, 40: 277–93.
Graham, L., Sweller, N. and Van Bergen, P. (2014) 'Detaining the usual suspects: Charting the use of segregated settings in New South Wales government schools in Australia', *Contemporary Issues in Early Childhood*, 13(1): 236–45.
Greenfield, T. (1975) 'Theory about organisations: A new perspective and its implications for schools', in M. Hughes (ed.), *Administering Education: International Challenges*. London: Athlone Press.

Gulson, K. (2005) 'Renovating urban identities: Policy, space and urban renewal', *Journal of Education Policy*, 20(2): 141–58.

Hargreaves, A. (2009) *The Fourth Way: The Inspiring Future for Educational Change*. Thousand Oaks, CA: Corwin.

Harris, K. and Graham, S. (1999) 'Programmatic intervention research: Illustrations from the evolution of self-regulated strategy development', *Learning Disability Quarterly*, 22: 251–62.

Held, D., McGrew, A., Goldblatt, D. and Perraton, J. (1999) *Global Transformations: Politics, Economics and Culture*. London: Polity Press.

Holmes, B. (1981) *Comparative Education: Some Considerations of Method*. London: Allen and Unwin.

Idea Store (2011) *About Us*. Available at: http://www.ideastore.co.uk/en/articles/about_us (accessed 20 April 2011).

Jackson, D. and Temperley, J. (2006) 'From professional learning community to networked learning community', paper given at the International Congress for School Effectiveness and Improvement (ICSI), Fort Lauderdale, 4 January.

Johnson, S. (1996) *Leading to Change: The Challenge of the New Superintendency*, San Francisco: Jossey Bass.

Knight, T. (1985) 'An apprenticeship in democracy', *The Australian Teacher*, 11(1): 5–7.

Knowles, M. (1970) *The Modern Practice of Adult Education: Andragogy Versus Pedagogy*. New York: Association Press.

Kolb, D. (1984) *Experiential Learning: Experience as the Source of Learning and Development*. New York: Prentice Hall.

Kopp, W. (1989) *An Argument and Plan for the Creation of the Teachers Corporation*, senior thesis, Woodrow Wilson School, Princeton University.

Kotter, J. (2012) *Leading Change*. Cambridge, MA: Harvard Business Review Press.

Kozol, J. (2005) *The Shame of the Nation: The Restoration of Apartheid Schooling in America*. New York: Crown Publishers.

Kraftl, P. (2013) *Geographies of Alternative Education: Diverse Learning Spaces for Children and Young People*. Bristol: Policy Press.

Lauglo, J. (1996) 'Forms of decentralisation and their implications for education', in J. Chapman, W. Boyd, R. Lander and D. Reynolds (eds), *The Reconstruction of Education: Quality, Equality and Control*. London: Cassell.

Lawn, M. (2006) 'Soft governance and the learning spaces of Europe', *Comparative European Politics: Rethinking European Spaces*, 4(2): 33–52.

Leat, D. and Nichols, A. (1997) 'Scaffolding children's thinking – doing Vygotsky in the classroom with National Curriculum assessment', paper presented at the British Educational Research Association Annual Conference, 11–14 September, University of York.

Lefebvre, H. (1991) *The Production of Space*, D. Nicholson-Smith, trans. Oxford: Basil Blackwell (originally published 1974).

Leithwood, K., Jantzi, D. and Steinbach, R. (1999) *Changing Leadership for Changing Times*. Buckingham: OUP.

Levin, B. (2001) *Reforming Education: From Origins to Outcomes*. London: Routledge Falmer.

Levin, B. (2005) *Governing Education*. Toronto: University of Toronto Press.

Levin, B. and Fullan, M. (2008) 'Learning about system renewal', *Educational Management, Administration and Leadership*, 36(2): 289–303.

Lingard, R. (2000) 'It is and it isn't: Vernacular globalisation', in N. Burbules and C. Torres (eds), *Globalisation and Education: Critical Perspectives*. London: Routledge. pp. 275–96.

Lugaz, C. and De Grauwe, A. (eds) (2010) *Schooling and Decentralization: Patterns and Policy Implications in Francophone West Africa*. Paris: International Institute for Educational Planning, UNESCO.

Luke, A. (2004) 'Teaching after the market: From commodity to cosmopolitan', *Teachers College Record*, 106(7): 1422–43.

Lundgren, U. and Mattsson, K. (1996) 'Decentralisation by or for school improvement', in J. Chapman, W. Boyd, R. Lander and D. Reynolds (eds), *The Reconstruction of Education: Quality, Equality and Control*. London: Cassell.

MacBeath, J. (2008) 'Stories of compliance and subversion in a prescriptive policy environment', *Education Management Administration and Leadership*, 36(1): 123–48.

MacBeath, J., O'Brien, J. and Gronn, P. (2012) 'Coping strategies among Scottish headteachers', *School Leadership and Management*, 32(5): 421–37.

Marginson, S. and Considine, M. (2000) *The Enterprise University*. Cambridge, UK: Cambridge University Press.

Martens, K. and Liebfried, S. (2008) 'The PISA story', *Atlantic Times*. Available at: http://www.atlantic-times.com/archive_detail.php?recordID=1132 (accessed 13 September 2015).

Martin, J. (2011) *Education Reconfigured: Culture, Encounter and Change*. New York: Routledge.

Marton, F. and Säljö, F. (1976) 'On qualitative differences in learning – 1: Outcome and process', *British Journal of Educational Psychology*, 46: 4–11.

McLaughlin, M. and Mitra, D. (2001) 'Theory-based change and change-based theory: Going deeper and going broader', *Journal of Educational Change*, 2(4): 301–23.

McPake, B., Ajuong, F., Forsberg, B., Liambillia, W. and Olenja, J. (2006) 'The Kenyan model of the Bamako initiative: Potential and limitations', *The International Journal of Health Planning and Management*, 8(2): 123–8.

Mehrotra, S. (1998) 'Education for all: Policy lessons from high-achieving countries', *International Review of Education*, 44(5/6): 461–84.

Miliband, D. (2004) *Personalised Learning: Building a New Relationship with Schools*. London: Department for Education and Skills.

Ministerial Council on Education (2008) *Australian Directions in Indigenous Education 2005–2008*. Canberra: Ministerial Council on Education, Employment, Training and Youth Affairs.

Ministry of Education, New Zealand (2011) *Overview of Operational Funding Components*. Government of New Zealand.

Ministry of Human Resource Development (MHRD) (2015) *Sarva Shiksha Abhiyan*. Delhi: Government of India.

Mitchell, C. and Sackney, L. (1998) 'Learning about organizational learning', in K. Leithwood and K.S. Louis (eds), *Organizational Learning in Schools*. Lisse, NL: Swets and Zeitlinger. pp. 177–203.

Morgan, M. (2010) *How Well Do Facts Travel? The Dissemination of Reliable Knowledge*. Cambridge: Cambridge University Press.

National Commission on Excellence in Education (1983) *A Nation at Risk*. Delhi: Government of India.

National Council for Teacher Education (NCTE) (1978) *Teacher Education Curriculum: A Framework*. Delhi: Government of India.

National Council for Teacher Education (NCTE) (2009) *National Curriculum Framework for Teacher Education*. Delhi: Government of India.

National Council of Educational Research and Training (NCERT) (2005) *National Curriculum Framework for School Education*. Delhi: Government of India.

National Council of Educational Research and Training (NCERT) (2011) *Leading the Change – 50 Years of NCERT*. New Delhi: NCERT.

National Council of Educational Research and Training (NCERT) (2014a) *BEd Curriculum*. New Delhi: NCERT.

National Council of Educational Research and Training (NCERT) (2014b) *DECCE*. New Delhi: NCERT.

National University of Educational Planning and Administration (NUEPA) (2013) *NUEPA at a Glance*. Delhi: NUEPA.

NIE (National Institute of Education) (2008) *Transforming Teacher Education – Redefined Professionals for 21st Century Schools*. Nanyang Technological University, Singapore.

Norwich, B. (2013) *Addressing Tensions and Dilemmas in Inclusive Education*. London: Routledge.

Nye, J. (2012) *The Future of Power*. New York: Public Affairs.

OECD (Organisation for Economic Cooperation and Development) (1992) *Education at a Glance*. Paris: OECD.

OECD (Organisation for Economic Cooperation and Development) (2005) *Teachers Matter – Attracting, Developing and Retaining Effective Teachers*. Paris: OECD.

OECD (Organisation for Economic Cooperation and Development) (2006) *Evidence in Education: Linking Research to Policy*. Paris: OECD.

OECD (Organisation for Economic Cooperation and Development) (2008) *Education at a Glance*. Paris: OECD.

OECD (Organisation for Economic Cooperation and Development) (2010a) *Education at a Glance 2010: OECD Indicators* [online]. Available at: www.oecd.org/edu/eag2010 (accessed 20 April 2011).

OECD (Organisation for Economic Cooperation and Development) (2010b) *OECD Reviews of Migrant Education – Closing the Gap for Immigrant Students*. Paris: OECD.

OECD (Organisation for Economic Cooperation and Development) (2015) *Education Policy Outlook 2015: Making Reforms Happen*. Paris: OECD.

Oliver, M. (1996) *Understanding Disability: From Theory to Practice*. Basingstoke: MacMillan.

Pandey, R. (2007) *Education in Emerging Indian Society*. Agra: Agrawal Publications.

Parsons, T. (1964) *Essays in Sociological Theory*. London: Free Press.

Pearson Foundation (2011) *Finland – Strong Performers and Successful Reformers in Education*. Available at: http://www.pearsonfoundation.org/oecd/finland.html (accessed 20 April 2011).

Phillips, D. and Schweisfurth, M. (2008) *Comparative and International Education: An Introduction to Theory, Method and Practice*. London: Continuum.

Piaget, J. (1962) *The Language and Thought of the Child*. London: Routledge and Kegan Paul.

Pritchett, L. and Pandey, V. (2006) 'Making primary education work for India's rural poor: A proposal for effective decentralization', *Social Development Papers – South Asia Series*, 95/ June.

Reed, M. (1992) *The Sociology of Organisations*. Hemel Hempstead: Harvester Wheatsheaf.

Rigg, J. (2007) *An Everyday Geography of the Global South*. Abingdon: Routledge.

Rix, J. (2015) *Must Inclusion be Special? Rethinking Educational Support within a Community of Provision: Current Debates in Educational Psychology*. London: Routledge.

Rizvi, F. and Lingard, B. (2010) *Globalising Education Policy*. Abingdon: Routledge.

Robertson, S. (2009) *Spatialising the Sociology of Education: Stand-points, Entry-points, Vantage-points*, Centre of Globalisation, Education and Societies, University of Bristol.

Rogers, E. (2003) *Diffusion of Innovation* (5th edn). New York: Free Press.

Rouse, M. and Florian, L. (1997) 'Inclusive education in the marketplace', *International Journal of Inclusive Education,* 1(4): 323–36.

Sahlberg, P. (2011a) *Finnish Lessons: What can the World Learn from Educational Change in Finland?* New York: Teachers College Press.

Sahlberg, P. (2011b) 'Developing effective teachers and school leaders: The case of Finland', in L. Darling-Hammond and R. Rothman (eds), *Teacher and Leader Effectiveness in High-Performing Education Systems.* Washington, DC: Alliance for Excellent Education; CA: Stanford Center for Opportunity Policy in Education. pp.13–21.

Schon, D. (2005) *The Reflective Practitioner: How Professionals Think in Action.* San Francisco: Jossey Bass.

Sexton, S. (1977) 'Evolution by choice' in C.B. Cox and R. Boyson (eds) *Black Paper 1977.* London: Temple Smith.

Shakespeare, T. (2014) *Disability Rights and Wrongs Revisited* (2nd edn). Abingdon: Routledge.

Shuangye, C. and Zheng, K. (2014) 'Why the leadership of change is especially difficult for Chinese principals: A micro-institutional explanation', *Journal of Organisational Change Management,* 27(3): 486–98.

Shukla, S. (1992) 'Pluralism and education in India – problems and possibilities', *Prospects,* 22(2): 195–206.

Silverman, D. (1971) *The Theory of Organisations: A Sociological Framework.* New York: Basic Books.

Slee, R. (2008) 'Beyond special and regular schooling? An inclusive education reform agenda', *International Studies in Sociology of Education,* 18(2): 99–116.

Slee, R. (2010) *The Irregular School – Exclusion, Schooling and Inclusive Education.* London: Routledge.

Smyth, J. (1989) 'A pedagogic and educative view of leadership', in J. Smyth (ed.), *Critical Perspectives on Educational Leadership.* London: Falmer.

Smyth, J. (ed.) (1993) *A Socially-critical View of the Self-managing School.* London: Falmer.

Street, L. and Timperley, R. (2005) *Improving Schools through Collaborative Enquiry.* London: Continuum.

Takala, M. (2007) 'The work of classroom assistants in special and mainstream education in Finland', *British Journal of Special Education,* 34: 50–57.

Taylor, C. (2011) 'Towards a geography of education', in J. Furlong and M. Lawn (eds), *Disciplines of Education: Their Role in the Future of Education Research.* London: Routledge.

Teese, R. and Polesel, J. (2003) *Undemocratic Schooling: Equity and Quality in Mass Secondary Education in Australia.* Carlton: Melbourne University Publishing.

Terano, M., Slee, R., Scott, D., Husbands, C., Naoum, D., Zotzmann, K. and Kingdon, G. (2011) *International Productive Practices in Education: Research Report to the International Best Practices Exchange Leading to Innovation in Sarva Shiksha Abhiyan (SSA) Project.* New Delhi: Save the Children.

Teach for America (TFA) (2015) *Our History* [online]. Available at: https://www.teach foramerica.org/about-us/our-story/our-history (accessed 9 November 2015).

Tharp, R. and Gallimore, R. (1991) 'A theory of teaching as assisted performance', in P. Light, S. Sheldon and M. Woodhead (eds), *Learning to Think: Child Development in Social Context,* Vol. 2. London: Routledge. pp. 42–61.

Titchkosky, T. (2007) *Reading and Writing Disability Differently: The Textured Life of Embodiment.* Toronto: University of Toronto Press.

Uddin, J. (2009) 'Community language provision in Tower Hamlets', *Community Languages,* 24.

UIS – UNESCO Institute of Statistics (2015) *Country Profiles – India.* Available at: http://www.uis.unesco.org/DataCentre/Pages/country-profile.aspx?code=IND&regioncode=40535 (accessed May 2015).

UNESCO (2009) *Policy Guidelines on Inclusion in Education.* Paris: United Nations Educational, Scientific and Cultural Organisation.

UNESCO (2014) 'EFA implementation: Teacher and resource management in the context of decentralization', seminar. Paris: UNESCO.

UNICEF (2007) *Child Poverty in Perspective: An Overview of Child Well-being in Rich Countries,* Innocenti Report Card 7. Florence, Italy: UNICEF Innocenti Research Centre.

Urry, J. (2007) *Mobilities.* Cambridge: Polity.

Walker, A., Bryant, D. and Lee, M. (2013) 'International patterns in principal preparation: Commonalities and variations in pre-service programmes', *Educational Management Administration and Leadership,* 41(4): 405–34.

Warnock Committee (1978) *Special Educational Needs: The Warnock Report.* London: Department for Education and Science.

White, J. and Barber, M. (1997) *Perspectives on School Effectiveness and School Improvement.* London: Institute of Education.

Whitty, G. (2002) *Making Sense of Education Policy: Studies in the Sociology and Politics of Education.* London: Paul Chapman Publishers.

Wigdortz, B. (2012) *Success Against the Odds: Five Lessons in how to Achieve the Impossible, the Story of Teach First.* London: Teach First.

Wilkins, R. (2010) 'The global context of local school leadership', in M. Coates (ed.), *Shaping a New Educational Landscape.* London: Continuum.

Wilkins, R. (2014) *Education in the Balance: Mapping the Global Dynamics of School Leadership.* London: Bloomsbury.

Wilkinson, R.G. and Pickett, K. (2009) *The Spirit Level: Why More Equal Societies almost always do Better.* London: Allen Lane.

Willms, D. (2003) 'Literacy proficiency of youth: Evidence of converging socio-economic gradients', *International Journal of Educational Research,* 39: 247–52.

Winch, C. (2014) 'Education and broad concepts of agency', *Educational Philosophy and Theory,* 48(6): 569–83.

World Bank (1997) *World Bank World Development Report 1997: The State in a Changing World.* Washington DC: World Bank.

World Bank (2005) *World Bank World Development Report 2005.* Washington DC: World Bank.

World Health Organisation (WHO) (2011) *World Health Statistics 2011.* New York: United Nations.

Yi-Fu Tuan (1996) 'Space and place: A humanistic perspective', in A. Agnew, D. Livingstone and A. Rogers (eds), *Human Geography: An Essential Anthology.* Oxford: Blackwell.

Author index

Ainscow, M. 86, 91, 95, 123, 124
Ajuong, F. 127
Alexander, W. 68, 123
Allan, J. 89, 96, 123
Annual Status of Education Report 25, 106, 123
Aristotle 58, 117, 123
Aspin, D. 64, 65, 123, 124
Aubrey, B. 49, 123

Ball, S. 5, 90, 123
Balshaw, M. 125
Bandura, A. 48, 123
Barber, M. 62, 79, 123, 130
Barnes, C. 88, 123
Barton, L. 88, 123, 124
Bauman, Z. 87, 123
Berryman, M. 123
Bhaskar, R. 89, 123
Bishop, R. 89, 102, 123
Black, P. J. 46, 93, 123
Black-Hawkins, K. 87, 123
Booth, T. 86, 95, 124
Borko, H. 43, 124
Bourdieu, P. 90, 124
Bourke, P. 91, 124
Bowles, S. 89, 124
Boyd, W. 66, 67, 73, 74, 123, 124, 126, 127
Brantlinger, E. 87, 124
Brook-Utne, B. 98, 124
Brundrett, M. 73, 124
Bruner, J. 44, 124
Bryant, D. 130

Caldwell, B. 64, 66, 124
Cardno, C. 74, 124
Chapman, J. 64, 66, 67, 73, 74, 124, 126, 127
Clifford, N. 103, 125
Cohen, P. 49, 123
Considine, M. 95, 127
Corbett, J. 88, 124
Czarniawska, B. 35, 36, 124

Danermark, B. 89, 123
Darling-Hammond, L. 93, 104, 124, 129
Department for Education 28, 67, 113, 119
Dorling, D. 89, 90, 125
Dunsan, J. 124
Dyson, A. 91, 92, 93, 96, 97, 102, 123, 125

Easton, D. 78, 125
Edge, K. 98, 125
Engeström, Y. 15, 125
Eskay, M. 89, 125
Etzioni, A. 78, 125

Farrell, P. 91, 125
Fitzgerald, T. 124
Florian, L. 89, 123, 129
Forsberg, B. 127
Foucault, M. 15, 125
Fullan, M. 8, 79, 104, 125, 126

Gagné, R. 49, 125
Gallimore, R. 47, 129
Gatrell, L. 103, 129
Giangreco, M. 91, 125
Gillborn, D. 125
Gintis, H. 89, 124
Glass, R. 92, 125
Glatter, R. 64, 125
Goldblatt, D. 126
Goldrick, S. 123, 125
Gough, N. 17, 125
Government of Queensland 104, 125
Graham, L. 88, 89, 90, 125
Graham, S. 51, 125
Greenfield, T. 78, 125
Gulson, K. 76, 126

Hargreaves, A. 93, 96, 126
Harris, K. 51, 125
Hayward, D. 64, 124

Held, D. 11, 126
Holmes, B. 60, 126
Husbands, C. 129

Idea Store 103, 126
Igbo, J. 125

Jackson, D. 42, 126
Jantzi, D. 126
Johnson, S. 63, 126
Jones, L. 125

Kerr, K. 125
Kihn, P. 123
Kingdon, G. 129
Knight, T. 106, 126
Knowles, M. 63, 126
Kolb, D. 50, 63, 126
Kopp, W. 27, 28, 126
Kotter, J. 7, 126
Kozol, J. 90, 126
Kraftl, P. 65, 126

Lauglo, J. 60, 82, 126
Lawn, M. 17, 126, 129
Leat, D. 47, 126
Lee, M. 130
Lefebvre, H. 77, 126
Leithwood, K. 62, 126, 127
Levin, B. 64, 79, 93, 126
Liambillia, W. 127
Liebfried, S. 127
Lingard, B. 11, 86, 126
Lingard, R. 64, 128
Luke, A. 95, 127
Lundgren, U. 65, 66, 127

MacBeath, J. 71, 74, 127
Marginson, S. 95, 127
Martens, K. 29, 127
Martin, J. 63, 127
Marton, F. 118, 127
Mattsson, K. 65, 66, 127
McGrew, A. 126
McLaughlin, M. 93, 127

McPake, B. 103, 127
Mehrotra, S. 98, 99, 127
Mercer, G. 88, 123
Miliband, D. 95, 127
Ministerial Council on Education 87, 127
Ministry of Human Resource Development (MHRD) 19, 116, 127
Mitchell, C. 43, 127
Mitra, D. 93, 127
Moffit, A. 123
Morgan, M. 34, 35, 36, 127

Naoum, D. 129
National Council for Teacher Education (NCTE) 19, 20, 54, 127
National Council of Educational Research and Training (NCERT) 19, 55, 56, 115, 127, 128
National University of Educational Planning and Administration (NUEPA) 19, 20, 114, 115, 116, 128
Nichols, A. 47, 126
NIE (National Institute of Education) 128
Norwich, B. 88, 128
Nye, J. 73, 128

O'Sullivan, D. 123
Obiyo, N. 125
Olenja, J. 127
Oliver, M. 88, 128
Onu, V. 125
Organisation for Economic Cooperation and Development (OECD) 91, 92, 98, 99, 100, 101, 102, 104, 128

Pandey, R. 21, 128
Pandey, V. 25, 128
Parsons, T. 16, 128
Passeron, J-C. 90, 124
Pearson Foundation 90, 128
Perraton, J. 126
Phillips, D. 128
Piaget, J. 120, 128
Pickett, K. 89, 90, 92, 105, 130
Polesel, J. 90, 129
Pritchett, L. 25, 128

Reed, M. 78, 128
Rigg, J. 76, 128
Rix, J. 87, 97, 128
Rizvi, F. 64, 86, 128
Robertson, S. 77, 128
Rogers, E. 35, 129
Rothman, R. 93, 124, 129
Rouse, M. 123
Ruelle, K. 91, 125

Sackney, L. 43, 127
Sahlberg, P. 31, 32, 35, 91, 129
Säljö, F. 118, 127
Schon, D. 40–2, 129
Schweisfurth, M. 11, 109, 111, 128
Scott, D. viii, 129
Sevon, G. 35, 36, 124
Shakespeare, T. 89, 129
Shuangye, C. 74, 129
Shukla, S. 106, 129
Silverman, D. 78, 129
Slee, R. 86, 88, 89, 90, 92, 96, 124, 125, 129
Smyth, J. 62, 63, 78, 129
Sommefeldt, T. 124
Spicer, B. 124
Steinbach, R. 126
Street, L. 43, 129
Sweller, N. 125

Takala, M. 91, 129
Taylor, C. 76, 129
Teach for America (TFA) 28, 129
Teese, R. 90, 129
Temperley, J. 42, 126
Terano, M. 64, 65, 113, 129
Tharp, R. 47, 129
Timperley, R. 43, 129
Titchkosky, T. 89, 130

Uddin, J. 103, 104, 130
Ugwuanyi, L. 125
UIS – UNESCO Institute of Statistics 106, 130
UNESCO 5, 87, 88, 106, 107, 127, 130
UNICEF 5, 92, 130
Urry, J. 76, 130

Van Bergen, P. 125

Walker, A. 74, 130
Warnock Committee 88, 130
West, M. 123
White, J. 62, 130
Wigdortz, B. 28, 31, 130
Wiliam, D. 46, 123
Wilkins, R. 60, 130
Wilkinson, R. 89, 90, 92, 105, 130
Willms, D. 90, 130
Winch, C. 39, 130
World Bank 21, 100, 130
World Health Organisation 89, 130

Yi-Fu Tuan 76, 130
Youdell, D. 90, 125
Youngs, H. 74, 124

Zheng, K. 74, 129
Zotzmann, K. 129

SUBJECT INDEX

Approach 9, 21, 26, 37, 45, 54, 60, 79, 96, 100
  Population-based 99, 100, 105
  Problem-based 99, 100, 105
Assessment for learning 37, 46
Autonomy 13, 15, 22, 23, 37, 53, 59–85

Bachelor of Education (BEd) 51–6
Bachelor of Elementary Education Programme (BEE) 51–6
Bureaucracy 3–4, 60

Central Board of Secondary Education 19, 81
Change catalyst 14–5
Council for the Indian Schools Certificate Examination (CISCE), India 19
Craft knowledge 38–9

Diploma in Early Childhood and Early Primary Teacher Education 51–6
Disability 75, 87, 88, 89
District Primary Education Programme, India 81
Diversity 86–108

Education Reform Act 1988, England and Wales 68, 69, 79
Education Act 1944, England 68
Effect
  Reform 5
  Socio-economic 88, 89, 92
Europe 2020 87

European Union 13, 113, 116
Exclusion 86–108
Executive technician 39
Experienced Principals' Development Programme (EPDP), New Zealand 74

General Certificate of Secondary Education (GCSE) 103
Global Education Reform Movement (GERM) 31–3

Hong Kong Certificate for Principalship 74
Human capital theory 1, 65

Immigration 99–100
Inclusive Education 86–108
Index for Inclusion 95
India 14–26
Inequality 91, 92, 93, 105, 106
Information and Communication Technology (ICT) 21
Institutionalisation 3, 4, 5, 6–7, 57–8
International Baccalaureate 19
Intervention 6

Knowledge 7, 8, 12, 16, 20, 21, 25, 26, 37, 38, 39

Leadership 59–85
Learning
  Conceptual 50
  Goal-oriented 48
  Instructional 49–50
  Meta-cognitive 51
  Peer 49
  Problem-solving 51

Learning Cycle 50
Learning Enhancement Programme (LEP), India 25
Learning outcomes 2, 25, 32, 45, 46, 47, 51, 61
Local Management of Schools (LMS) 69, 70
London Centre for Leadership in Learning (UK) 72

Ministry of Human Resource Development (MHRD), India 19, 20, 23, 24, 116
Model
  Multi-level 79, 110–111
  Ontario 8
  Policy borrowing 1–13, 109–122
  Policy learning 1–13, 109–122
  Professional development 10
  Quasi-market 9–10
  Reform 9–11
  Social participation 10
  Teacher-as-local-expert 43
  Top-down 9
Moral agent 58

National College for School Leadership (NCSL), England 72, 73
National Council for Teacher Education (NCTE), India 19, 20, 21, 23
National Council of Educational Research and Training (NCERT), India 23

National Curriculum Framework for School Education (2005), India 19, 21
National Curriculum Framework for Teacher Education (2009), India 19, 21
National Literacy Strategy, England 77
National Policy on Education (NPE), India 18, 19, 20, 81
National Professional Qualification for Headship (NPQH), England 72, 73
National University of Educational Planning and Administration (NUEPA), India 19, 20
New York City Aspiring Principals Programme 74

Office for Standards in Education (OFSTED), England 70, 116
Organisation for Economic Cooperation and Development (OECD) 91, 92, 98, 99, 100, 101, 102, 104, 128
Organisation for European Economic Cooperation (OEEC) 28–29

Pedagogy 47–51
Policy
  Borrowing 1–13, 109–122
  Learning 1–13, 109–122
Politics 34, 64

Productive practices 12–3, 64–5, 105, 108, 113, 117, 118, 119, 120, 125
Professional development 10, 41–3, 73
Professionalism 20, 60, 86, 93
Programme for International Student Assessment (PISA) 15, 28–30
Pupil–teacher ratio 24, 25

Qualified Teacher Status (QTS), England 104

Reflective practitioner 40–2
Reflexivity 41, 42
Reform
  Education 5, 7–11
  Effort 3, 74, 96
Right to Education Act (RTE), India 21, 24

Sarva Shiksha Abhiyan (SSA) 23–6, 81–4, 113, 116, 120
Save the Children
  England 113
  India 64, 113, 114, 115, 116, 118
Scaffolding 38, 45, 47–8
Scheduled castes 23, 24, 84, 86
Scheduled tribes 23, 84, 105
School
  Effectiveness 60, 61, 81
  Government 67, 68, 81, 118
  Private 19, 25, 81, 83
  Self-managing 66
School Contact Programme 52
Special Educational Needs (SEN) 88, 90, 96

Standards 2, 37–58
  Curriculum 37–58
  Pedagogic 37–58

Targeted Funding for Educational Achievement (TFEA) 97, 98
Teach First, UK 28, 31, 130
Teach for All 28, 30, 31, 32, 33, 34
Teach for America 28, 129
Teacher Training 37–58
  In-service 37–58
  Pre-service 37–58
  Programme 37–58
  Trainer 37–58
Theory of
  Human capital 1, 60, 65, 92
  Learning 45, 118, 120
  Transfer 11, 12, 13, 22, 37, 39, 44, 45, 47, 48, 56, 57, 81, 100, 109–22

United Nations Children's Fund (UNICEF) 5, 81, 92, 130
United Nations Educational, Scientific and Cultural Organisation (UNESCO) 5, 20, 87, 88, 106, 107, 127, 130
University of
  Delhi 52
  London, Institute of Education 72, 113, 115, 125, 130

World Bank 5, 21, 100, 125, 130
World Health Organisation (WHO) 89, 130